Banjo Backup Licks  Book with Video & Audio

Includes the following video lessons:

- **Lesson 1 - Using Basic Backup Licks**
- **Lesson 2 - More Basic Backup Licks**
- **Lesson 3 - Backing Up Vocals**
- **Lesson 4 - Using Rolls For Backup**
- **Lesson 5 - Using Rolls For Backup #2**
- **Lesson 6 - Creating Your Own Backup**

About this Video & Book

This booklet contains all the banjo tablature required for all six lessons. At the bottom of each page you'll see the name of the particular lesson and the page number referred to in the video. The lessons and printed material are the same content and length as the original lessons available as downloads on BanjoCompass.com.

Special Note to Students

If you need help with tuning your banjo, watch the free video lesson on tuning at our website BanjoCompass.com. If you need additional assistance with tuning, take your banjo to your local music store and ask them to show you how to tune.

From time to time Geoff Hohwald, the on-screen banjo instructor, will refer to other lessons which are not on this video but are available for viewing on the website. Geoff has created many free video banjo lessons on topics such as tuning, scales, and chords, which are very helpful and can be viewed by visiting the website:

For Video & Audio Access, go to this address on the web:
http://cvls.com/extras/bpb3/

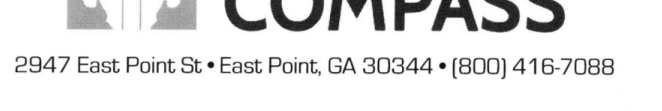

2947 East Point St • East Point, GA 30344 • (800) 416-7088

About the Instructor

Geoff Hohwald began playing banjo in 1964 in Columbus, Ohio which was a "hot bed of bluegrass" at the time. While there, Geoff studied banjo under John Hickman. He performed with many other great musicians there including Bill Monroe's last two guitar players Tom Ewing and Wayne Lewis. Other Musicians that Geoff played with in the Columbus area were Red Allen, Sandy Rothman, Sid Campbell, Dave Evans, Frank Wakefield, Hylo Brown, Buddy Thomas, The Fields Brothers, Landon Messer, Earl Taylor and Brian Aldridge.

Since coming to Atlanta, Geoff has played with Bear Creek in Underground Atlanta, at the Alliance Theatre for the Robber Bridegroom, with the Atlanta Pops Orchestra, and is one of the founding members of the Greater Atlanta Bluegrass Band.

Geoff is mostly known around the country for his banjo teaching materials which are sold world wide including the popular *Banjo Primer*. He has been collecting vintage instruments for years and has owned or played all of the classic bluegrass instruments and has helped many musicians in the southeast area obtain classic instruments.

TABLE OF CONTENTS

Thoughts on Backup iv

Backup Licks and Rolls 1 - Using Basic Backup Licks 1-5

Backup Licks and Rolls 2 - More Basic Backup Licks 6-10

Backup Licks and Rolls 3 - Backing Up Vocals 11-14

Backup Licks and Rolls 4 - Using Rolls For Backup 15-22

Backup Licks and Rolls 5 - Using Rolls For Backup #2 22-31

Backup Licks and Rolls 6 - Creating Your Own Backup 32-44

Thoughts on Backup Playing

By Geoff Hohwald

In the old days, when bluegrass bands performed around one microphone, you literally had to "back up" when someone else was taking a solo. You either would move to the back or be pushed back! That automatically had the effect of reducing the volume of the player who backed away from the microphone. To this day, regulating your volume so as not to overpower the lead instrument or vocalist is one of the most important focuses of backup.

Unlike backup, when playing lead, the banjo player has the spotlight to himself and can play memorized solos. The majority of his or her time is spent learning these arrangements. The other musicians in the band have to adjust to the banjo solo just as the banjo player has to adjust to the other musicians when they are taking a break.

When playing backup or non-lead parts, the banjo player operates out of chord positions with the left hand. The right hand tends to play repetitive patterns. This includes licks, lead-in runs, percussive playing of chord formations, and runs that encompass large parts of the fingerboard, moving from one chord inversion to another or from one chord to another. The more precise and even these patterns are, the better the backup fits in with what the other musicians are doing. Therefore, to learn backup, the best way is to identify and isolate the various licks, chord shapes, and patterns that you want to use and practice them over and over until you master them.

Listening is another important component of backup. You need to know where you are in the song at all times. You must know the chord progression of the song as well as the melody and the phrasing. This also includes knowing when the singer or lead player makes a mistake by holding a particular note too many beats or forgetting where they are. As a backup player, your job is to stay with them through thick and thin and make adjustments to make them sound as good as they possibly can.

Because the banjo player is constantly reacting to what is going on with the other instruments he is making split second decisions. As a result, he or she needs to know and be able to use each lick and chord form almost subconsciously.

Here are some suggestions when using The Back Up Video Lessons:

1. Learn each back up technique or pattern one at a time and master it.

2. Watch each section of the video a few times before starting to practice a new technique pattern or lick.

3. Learn how to use a metronome and use the metronome to help gradually increase your speed.

4. Use the menu system in the bottom right hand corner of the video to bypass explanations and quickly locate what you want to work on.

5. Learn the three major chord positions and the corresponding minor and 7th positions everywhere on the neck.

6. Focus on clarity, smoothness and being in time. If your instrument stands out, you are playing either too loud, too many notes, or not playing smoothly and evenly.

7. Practice by playing each new technique or lick in all of the places in the song that it will go.

8. As you master each technique, play it along with the video and the included mp3 tracks that come as part of your download.

9. As you learn more licks and techniques, practice them in pairs until you can use them anywhere.

10. Before starting to practice with a track, listen to it along with a lead sheet or template and make sure you know the basic chord progression. Listen to the point that you can sing along with the first verse and chorus. Your singing does not have to be a thing of beauty. You just need to know the phrasing. This will help you cement the chord changes and know where the spaces are where the singer is taking a breath.

11. Record yourself playing and listen back to it. If you or a friend have some sort of a video camera, you can record yourself playing along with tracks or the metronome and listen back to it. If you do not have a video camera ask around, I'll bet one of your friends or relatives has an old VHS camera in the closet. These are really cheap and will work just fine.

12. Go to jam sessions in your area to practice and network with other musicians.

Banjo Backup Licks & Rolls

The Lessons

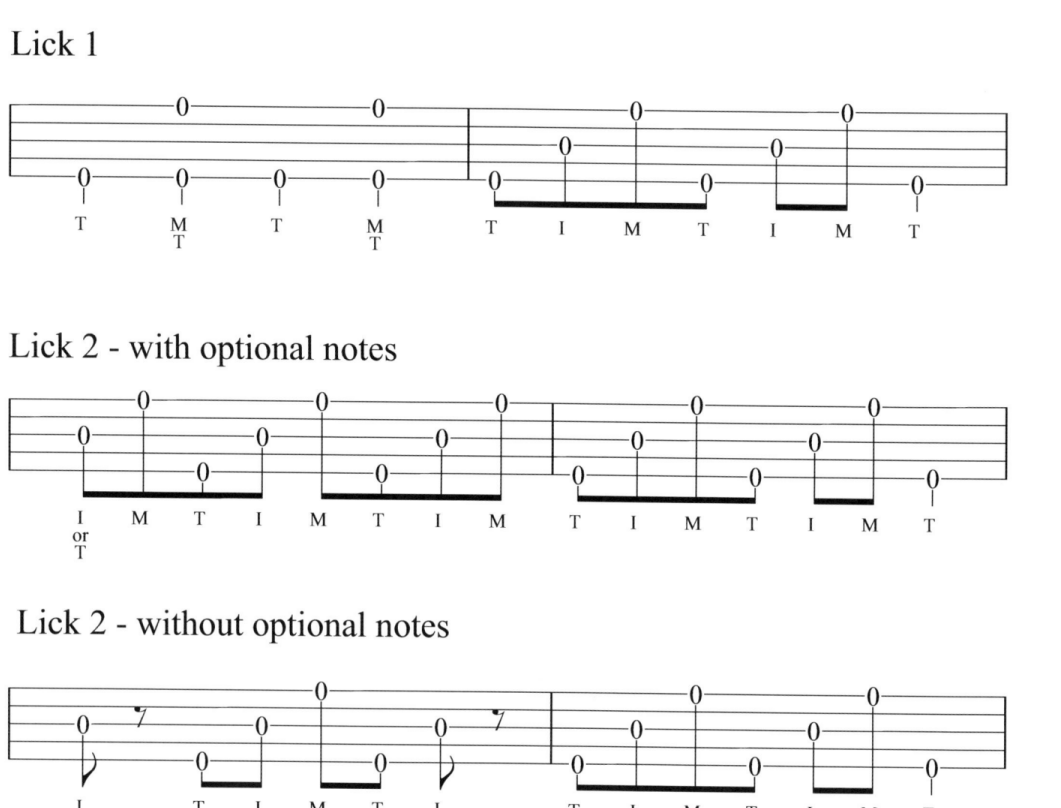

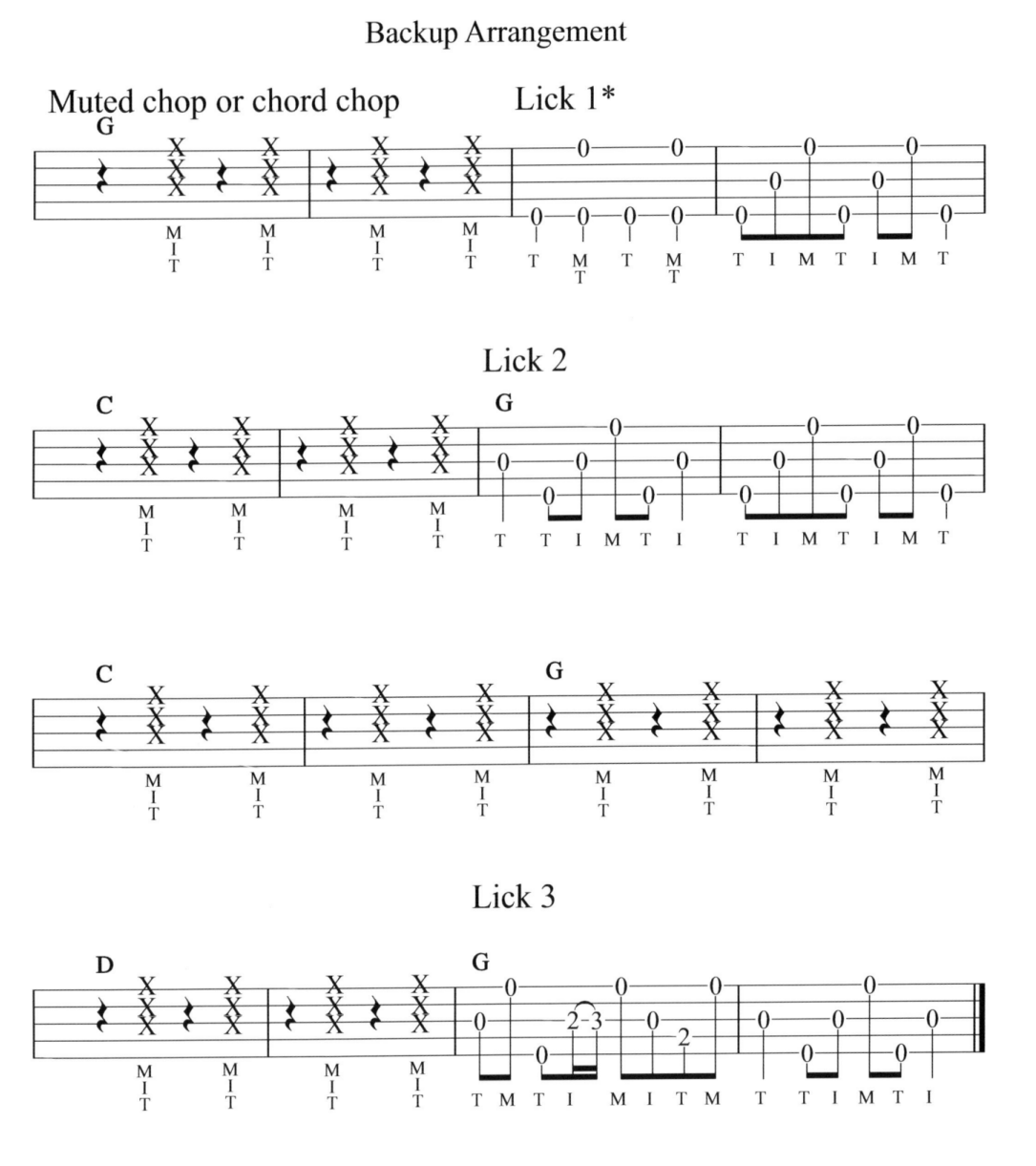

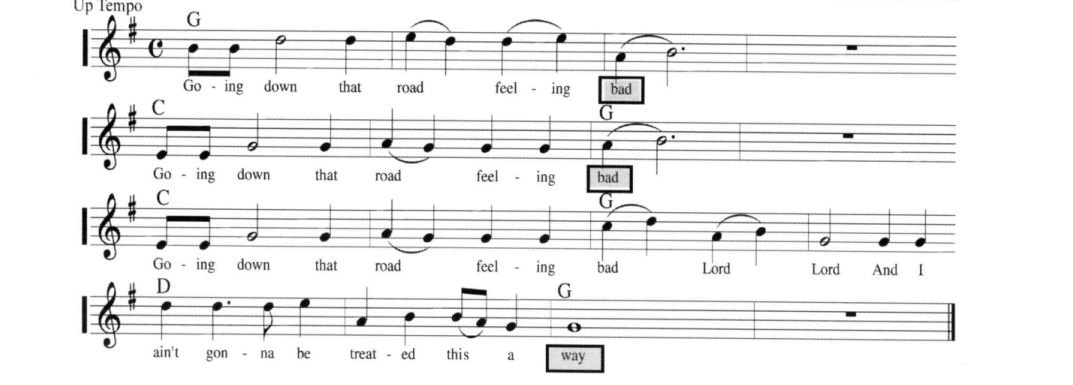

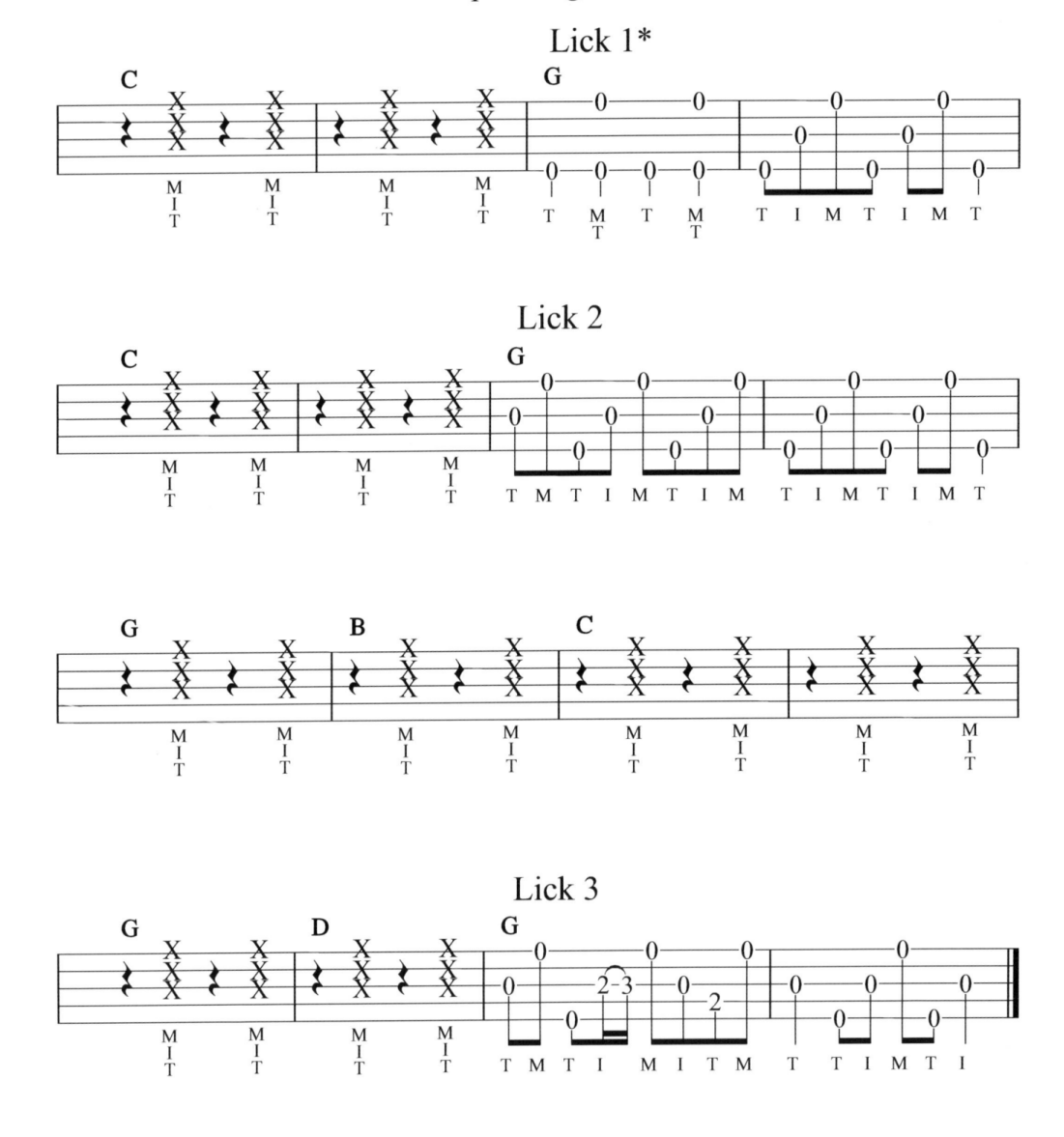

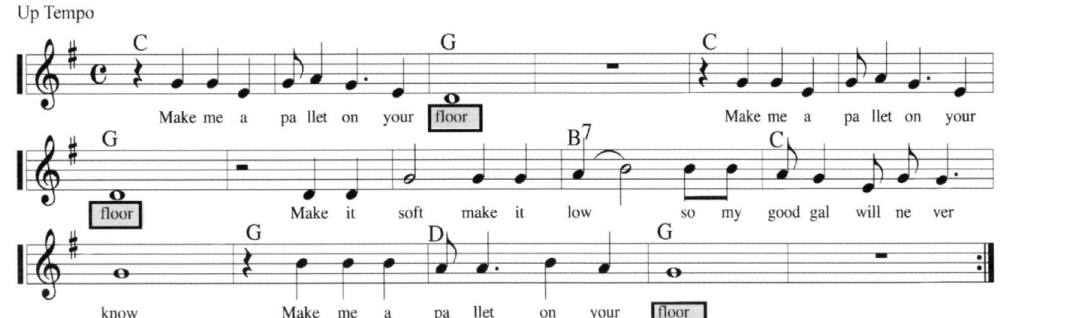

Chorus

Make me a pallet on your floor
Make me a pallet on your floor
Make it soft, make it low so my good gal will never know
Make me a pallet on your floor

These blues are everywhere I see
Weary blues are everywhere I see
Blues all around me, everywhere I see
Nobody's had these blues like me
Chorus

Come all you good time friends of mine
Come all you good time friends of mine
When I had a dollar you treated me just fine
Where'd you go when I only had a dime
Chorus

I'd be more than satisfied
If I could catch a train and ride
When I reach Atlanta and have no place to go
Won't you make me a pallet on your floor
Chorus

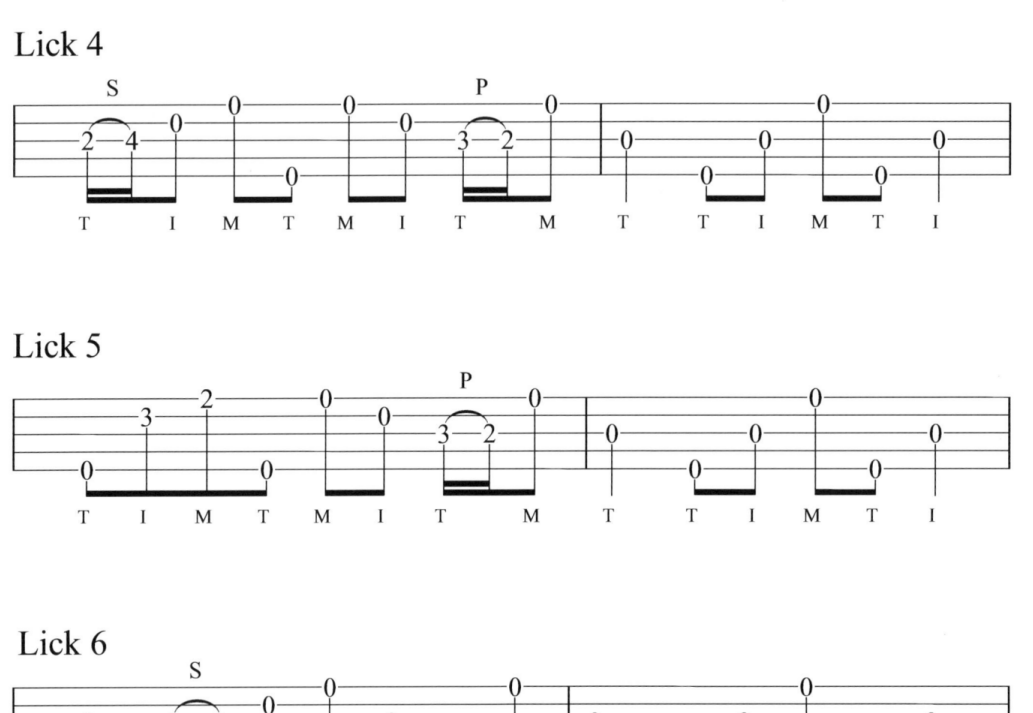

Little Maggie

Traditional

Yonder stands little Maggie with a dram glass in her hand
She's passing away her troubles by courting another man

Oh how can I ever stand it just to see them two blue eyes
Shining in the moonlight like two diamonds in the skies

Pretty flowers were made for blooming, pretty stars were made to shine
Pretty women were made for loving, Little Maggie was made for mine

Last time I saw little Maggie she was setting on the banks of the sea
With a forty-four around her and a banjo on her knee

Lay down your last gold dollar, lay down your gold watch and chain
Little Maggie's gonna dance for Daddy, listen to this old banjo ring

I'm going down to the station with my suitcase in my hand
I'm going away for to leave you, I'm going to some far distant land

Go away, go away little Maggie, go and do the best you can
I'll get me another woman, you can get you another man

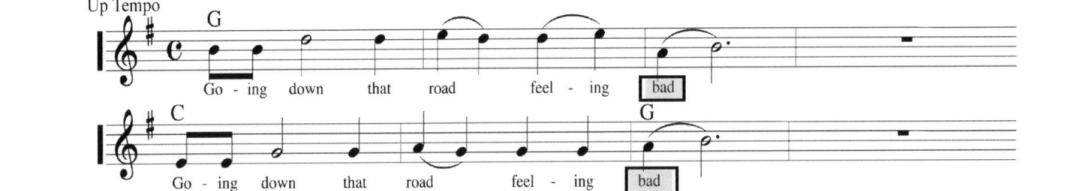

Chorus

Going down that road feeling bad
Bad luck's all I ever had
Going down that road feeling bad, Lord, Lord
And I ain't gonna be treated this a way

Got me way down in jail on my knees
This jailer, he sure is hard to please
Feed me on corn bread and peas, Lord, Lord
And I ain't gonna be treated this a way

Sweet mama won't buy me no shoes
She's left with these lonesome jail house blues
My sweet Mama won't buy me no shoes, Lord, Lord
And I ain't gonna be treated this a way

These two dollar shoes they hurt my feet
The jailer won't give me enough to eat
These two dollar shoes they hurt my feet, Lord, Lord
And I ain't gonna be treated this a way

I'm going where the climate suits my clothes
I'm going where these chilly winds don't blow
I'm going where the climate suits my clothes, Lord, Lord
And I ain't gonna be treated this a way

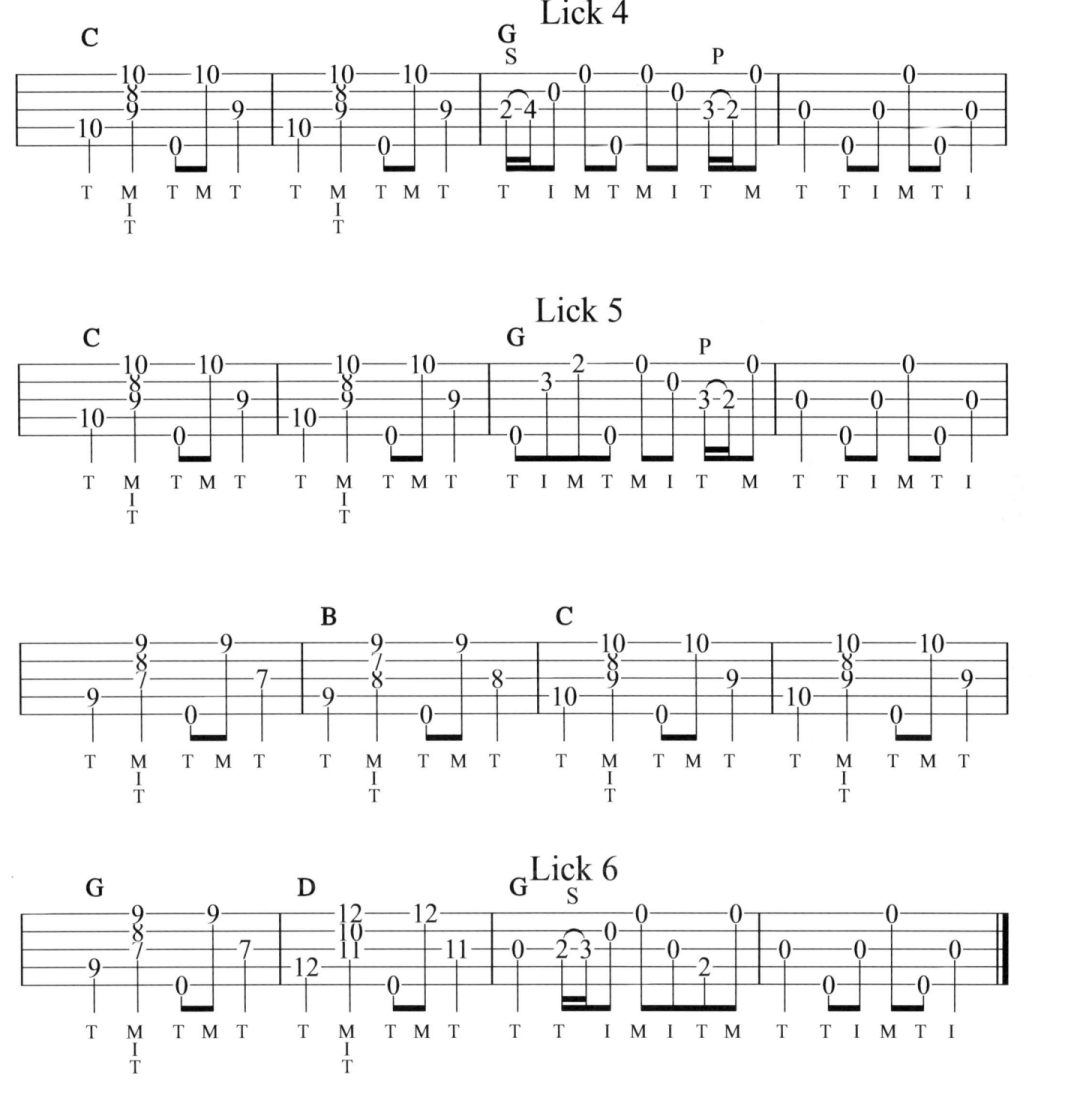

Pallet On Your Floor

Traditional

Up Tempo

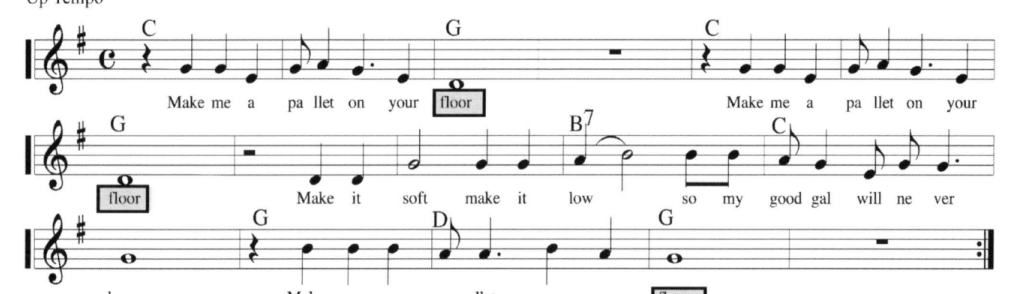

Chorus

Make me a pallet on your floor
Make me a pallet on your floor
Make it soft, make it low so my good gal will never know
Make me a pallet on your floor

These blues are everywhere I see
Weary blues are everywhere I see
Blues all around me, everywhere I see
Nobody's had these blues like me
Chorus

Come all you good time friends of mine
Come all you good time friends of mine
When I had a dollar you treated me just fine
Where'd you go when I only had a dime
Chorus

I'd be more than satisfied
If I could catch a train and ride
When I reach Atlanta and have no place to go
Won't you make me a pallet on your floor
Chorus

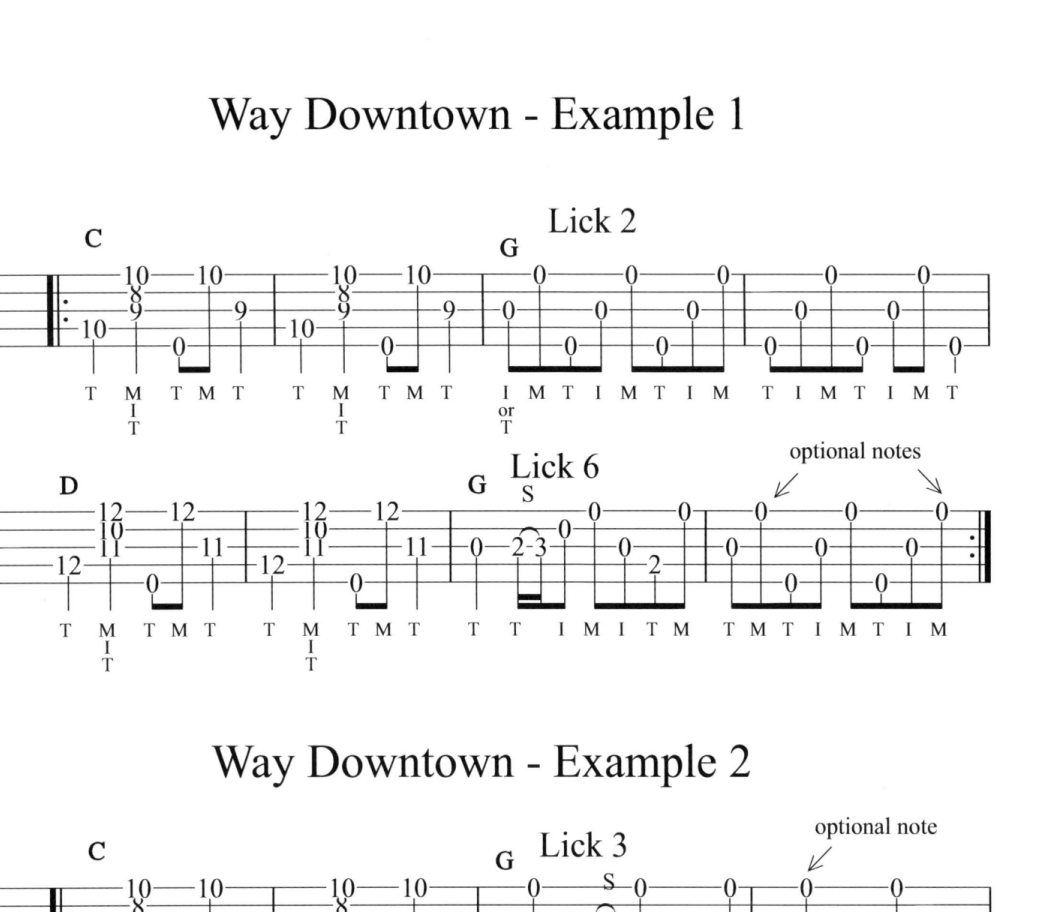

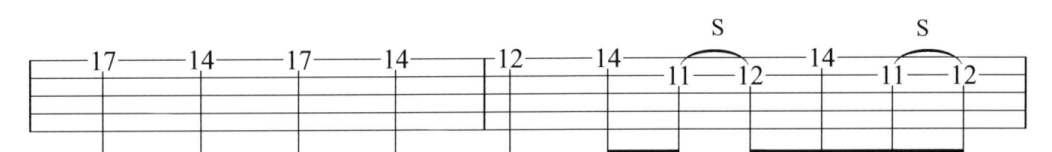

Way Downtown - Example 3

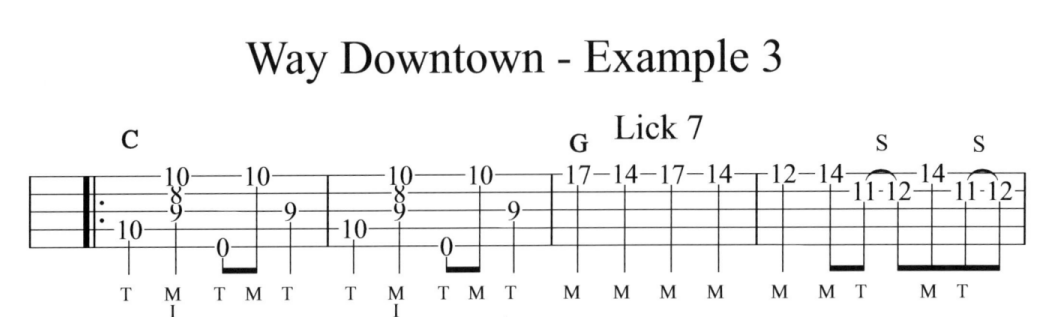

Backup Licks & Rolls 3 • Page 2

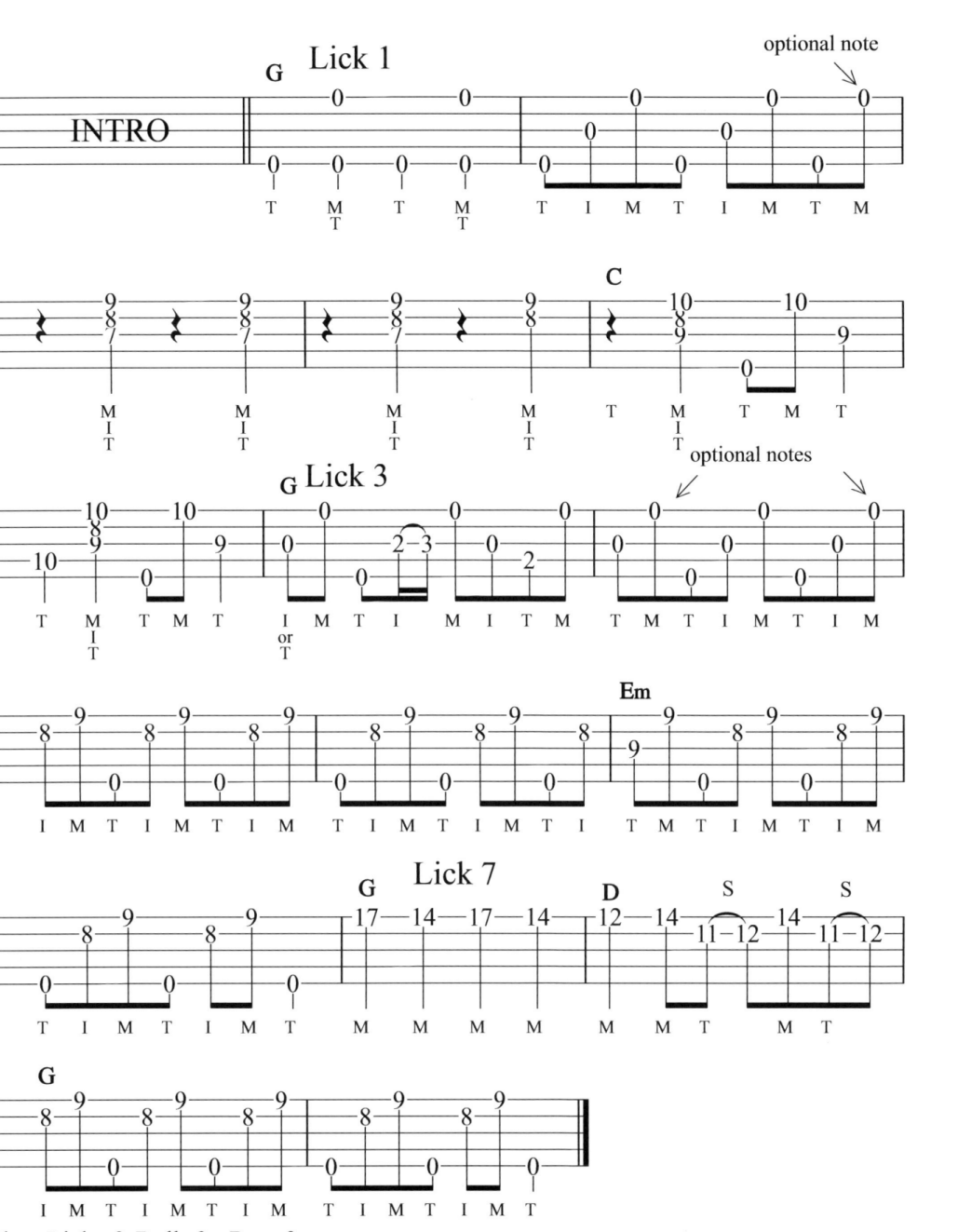

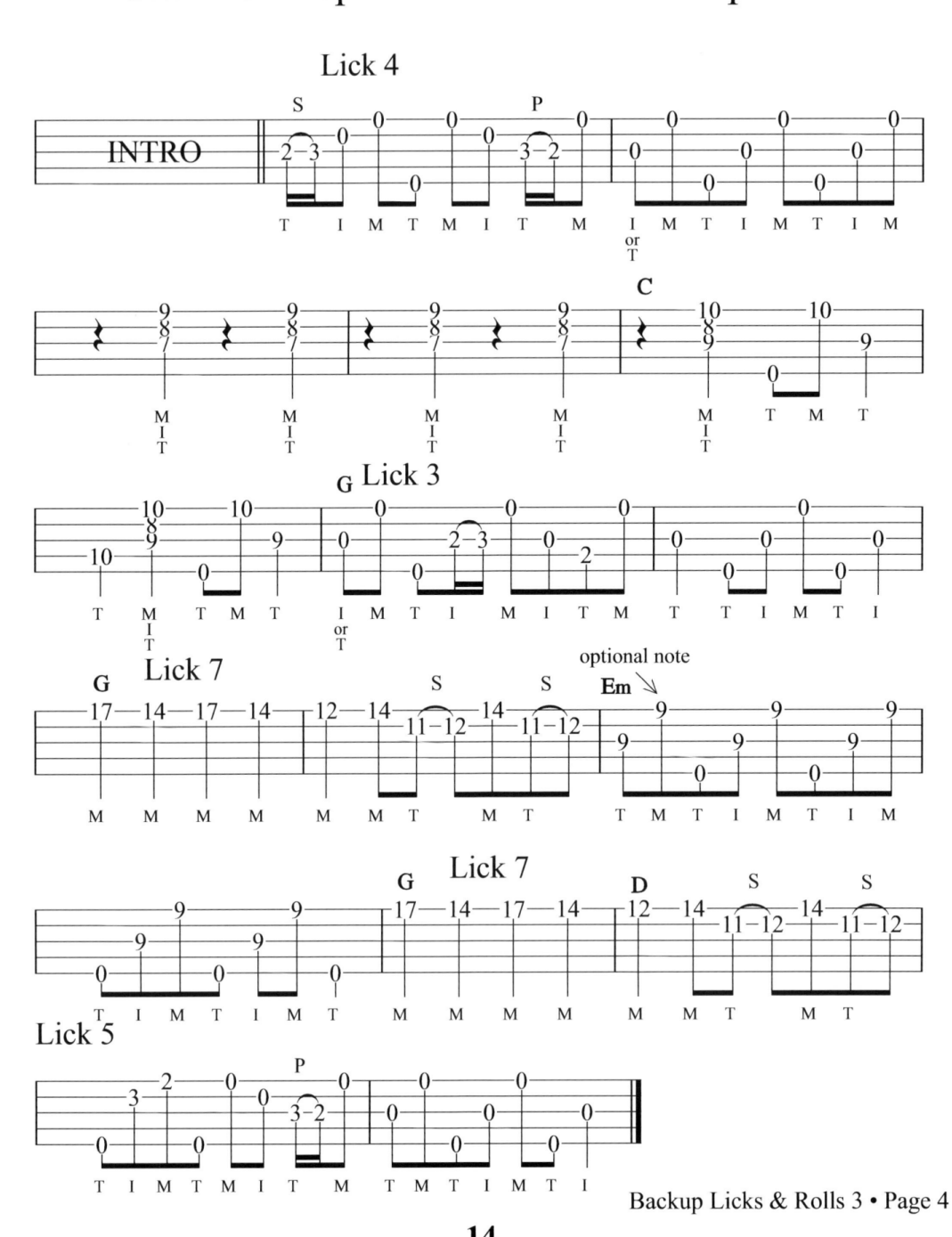

Backup Licks & Rolls Lesson 4

Section 1 - Review

7 Note Roll 1:40

Down the Neck Chord Shapes Used:

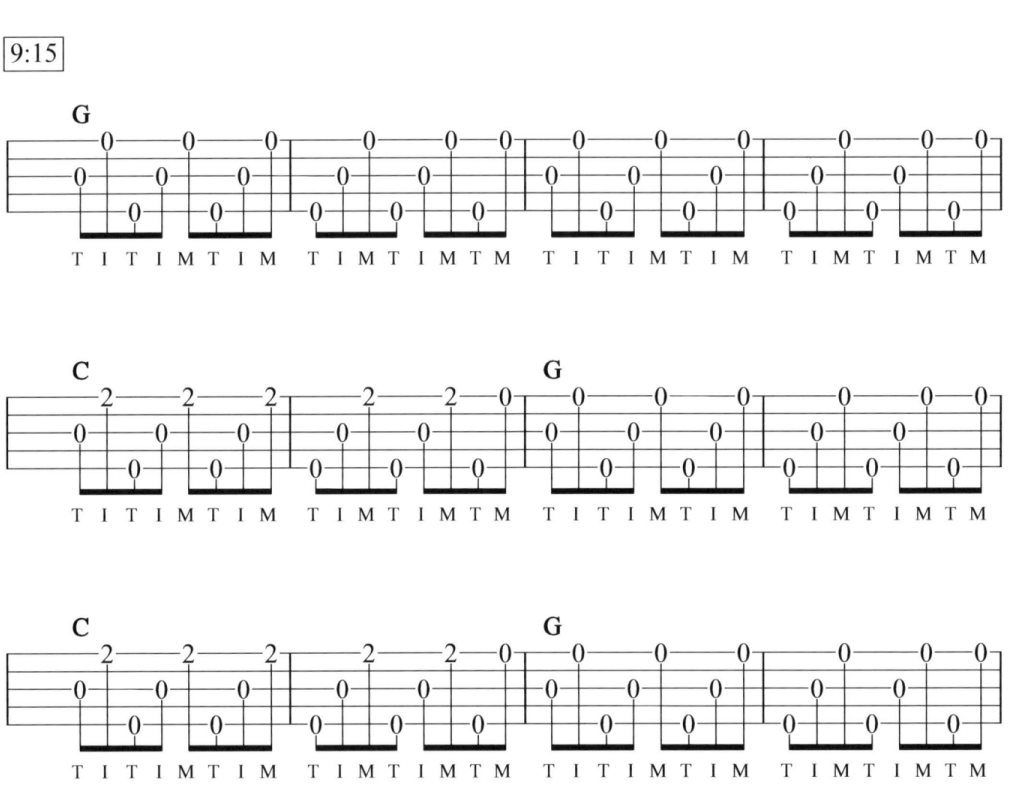

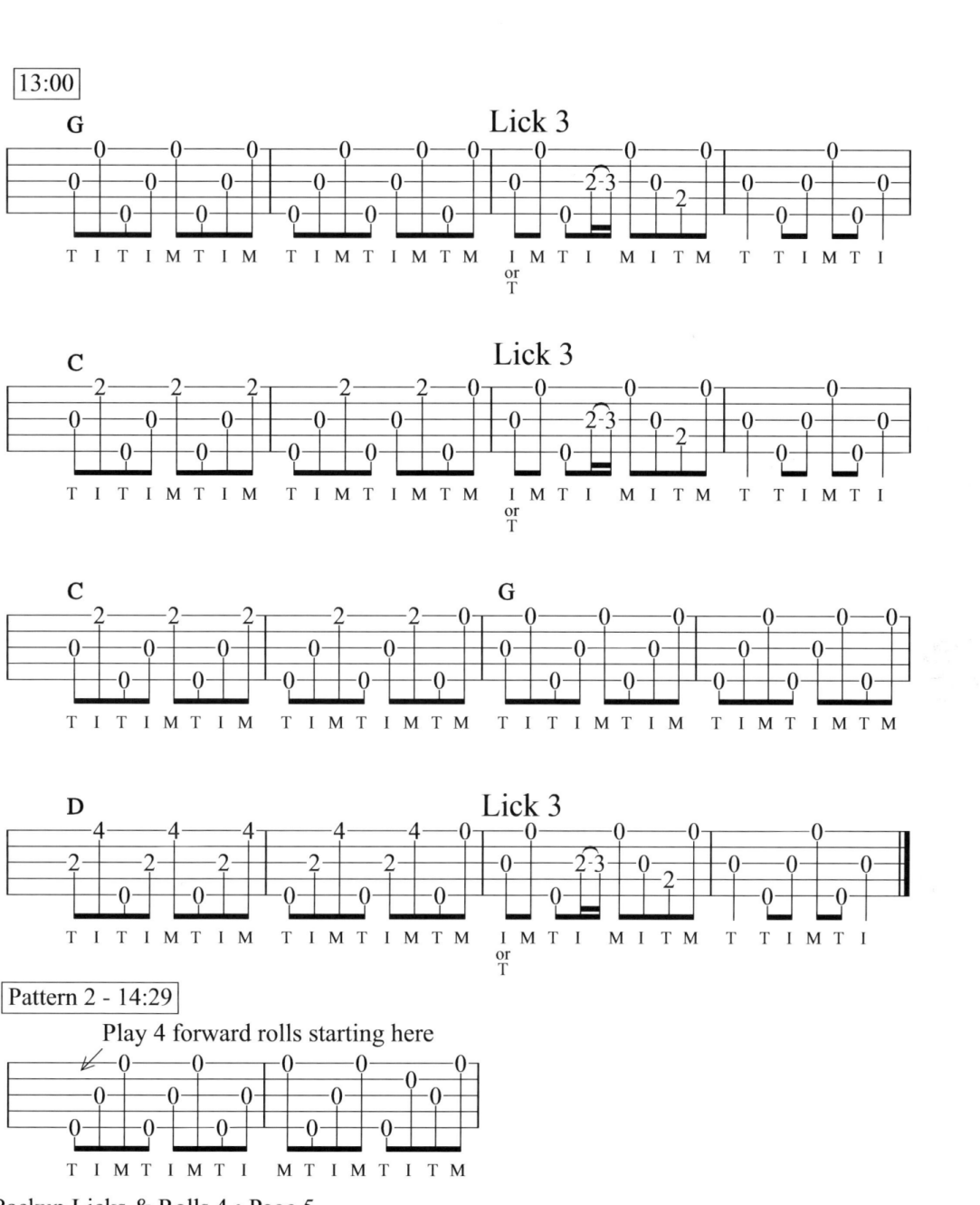

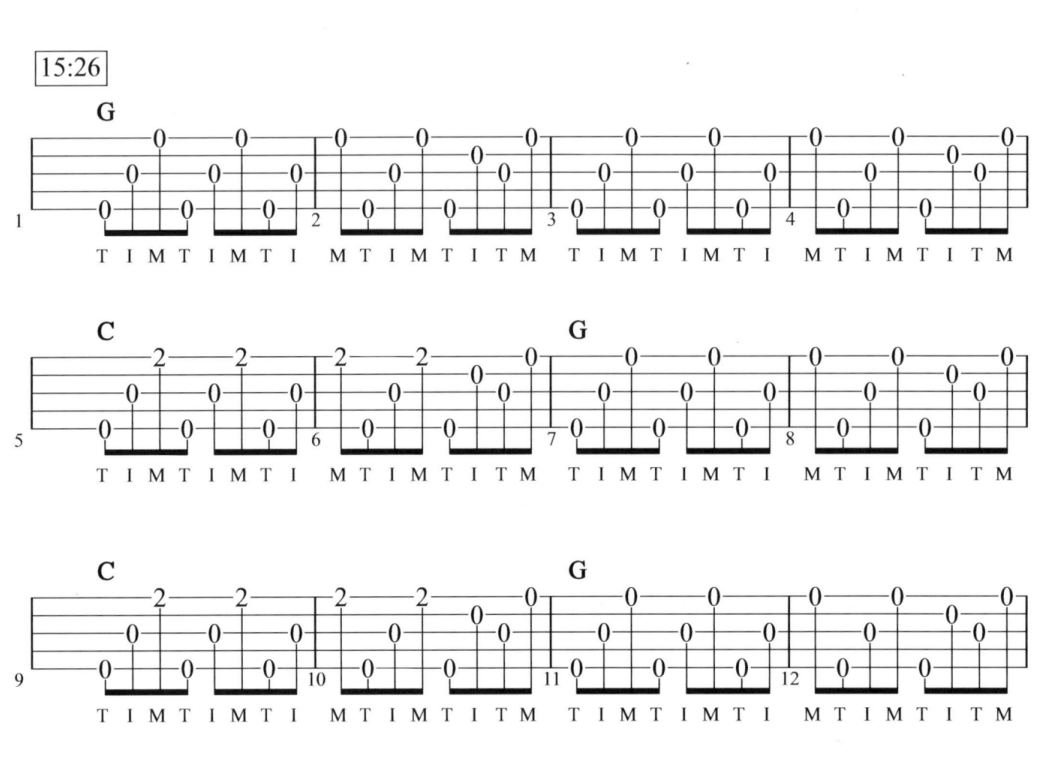

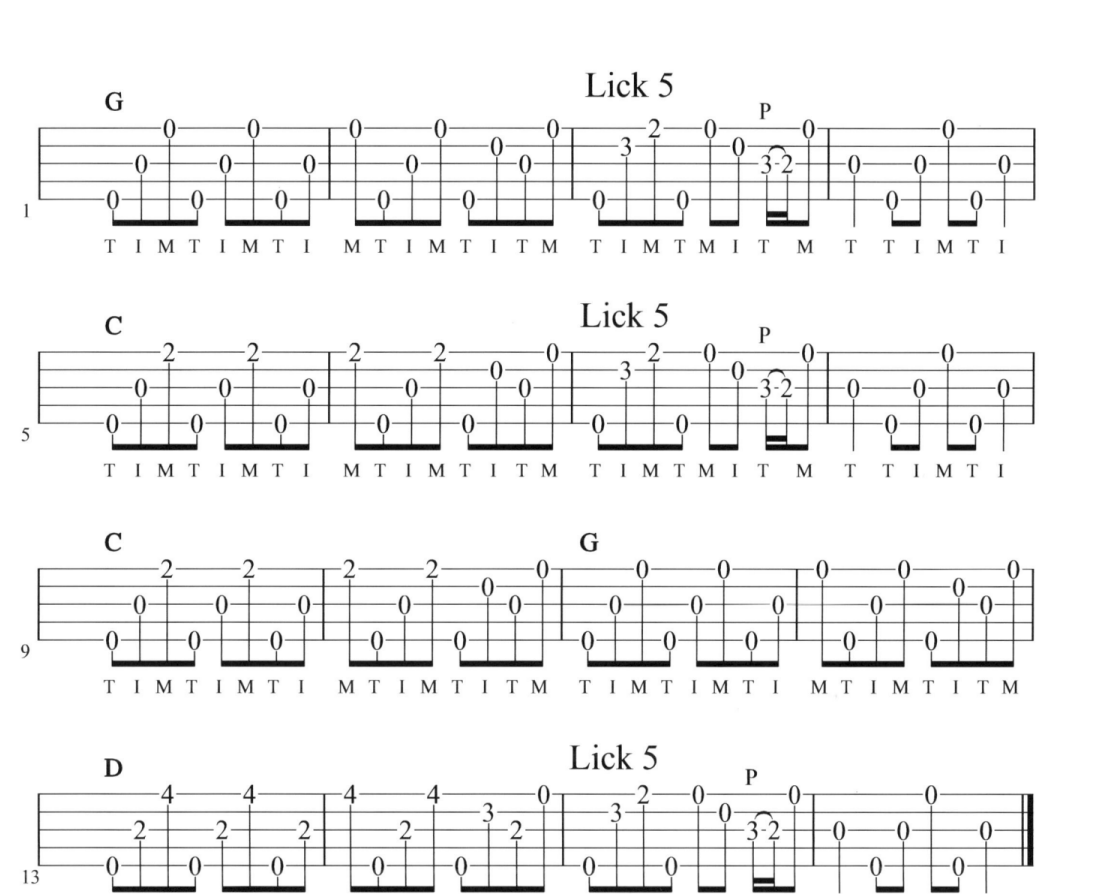

Backup Licks & Rolls Lesson 5

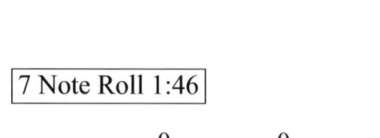

Pattern 2 and 7 Note Roll

Pattern 2 and 7 Note Roll with Chord Changes

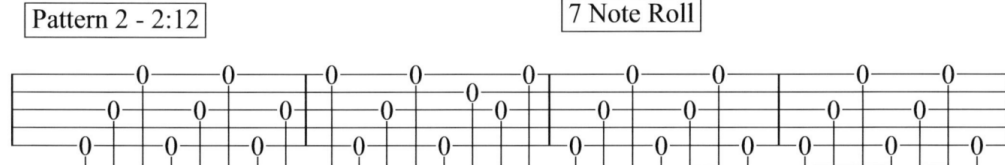

Backup Licks & Rolls 5 • Page 1

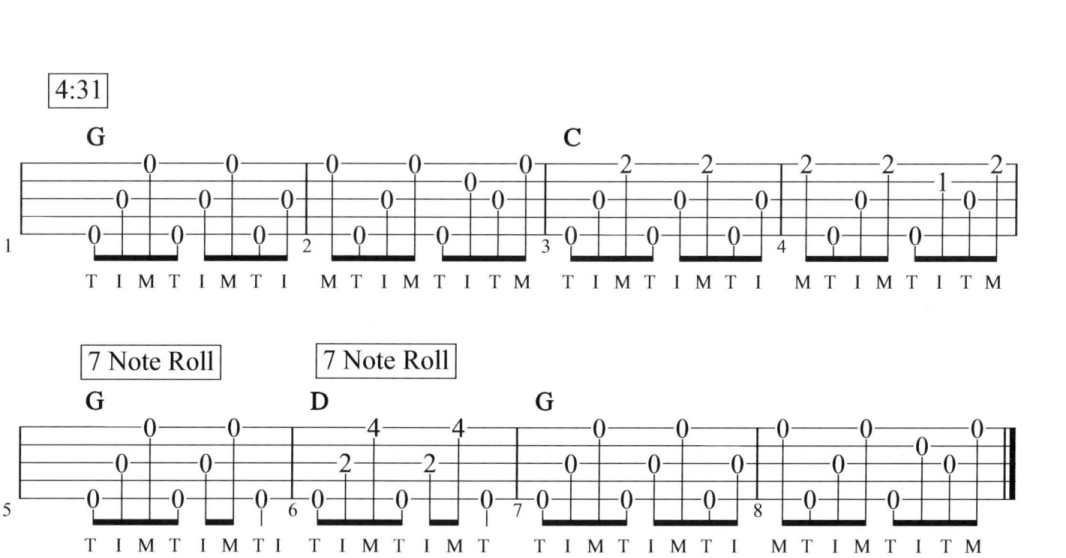

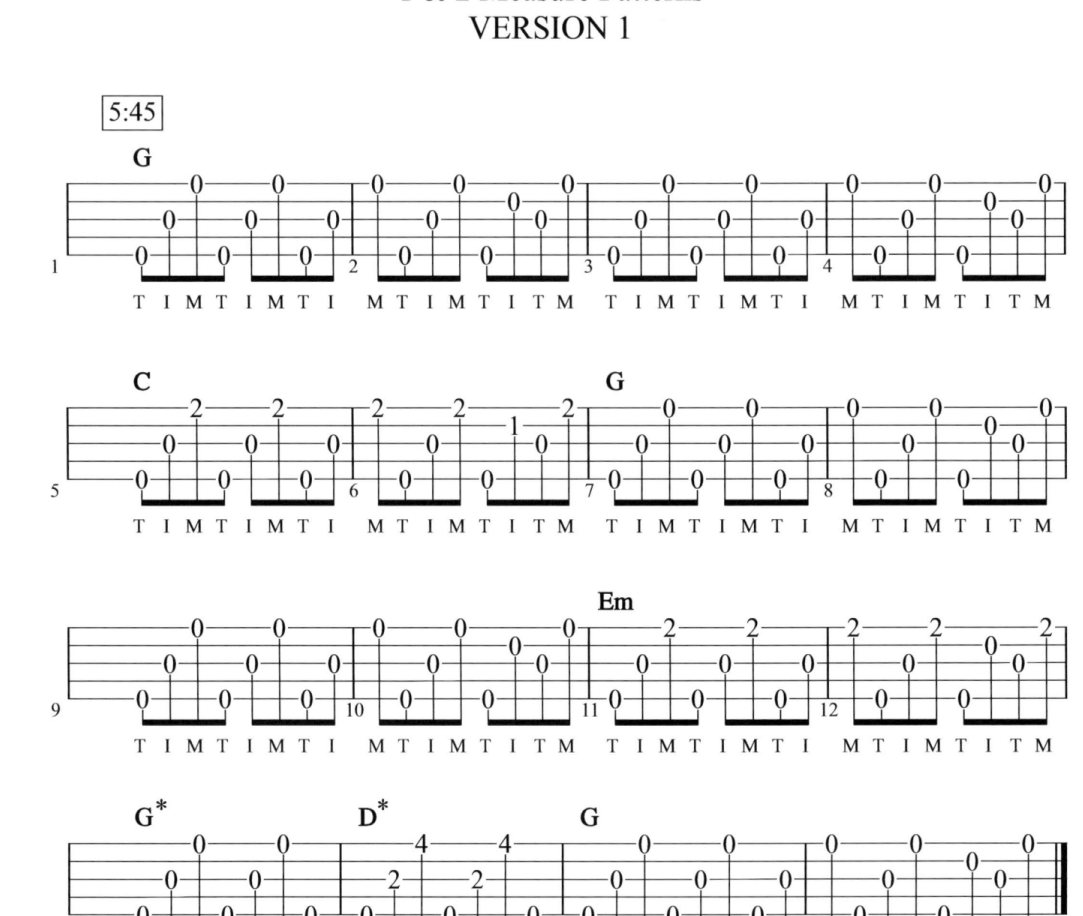

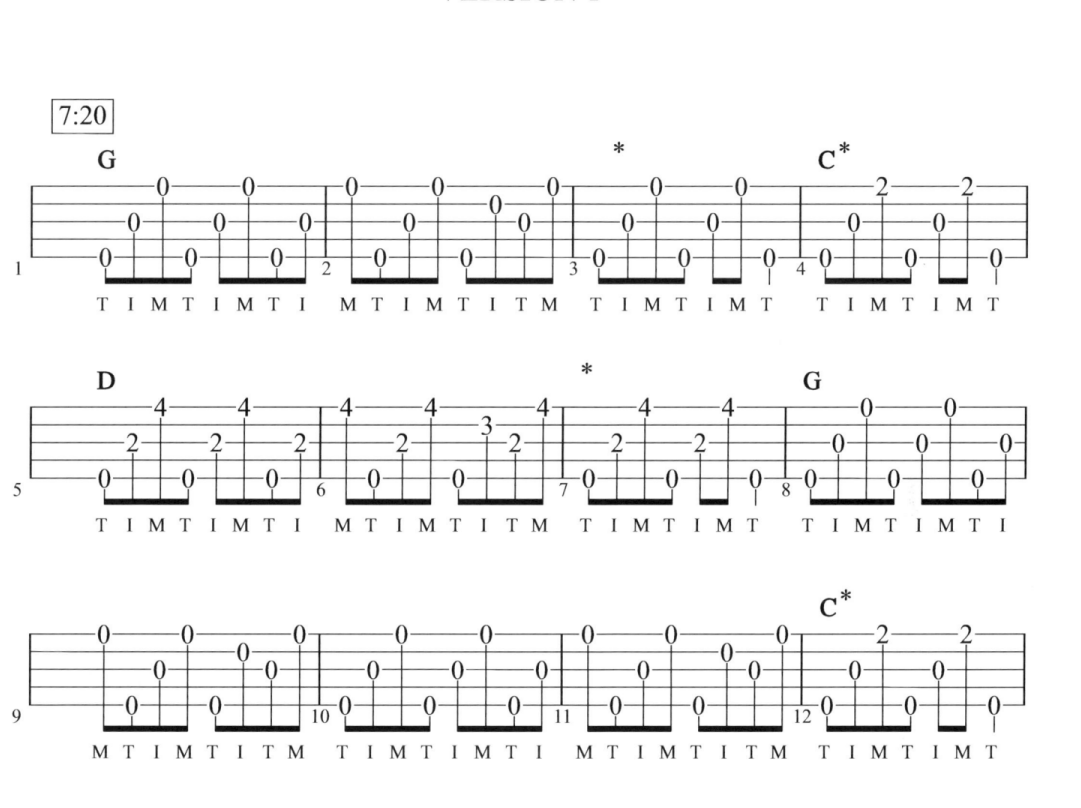

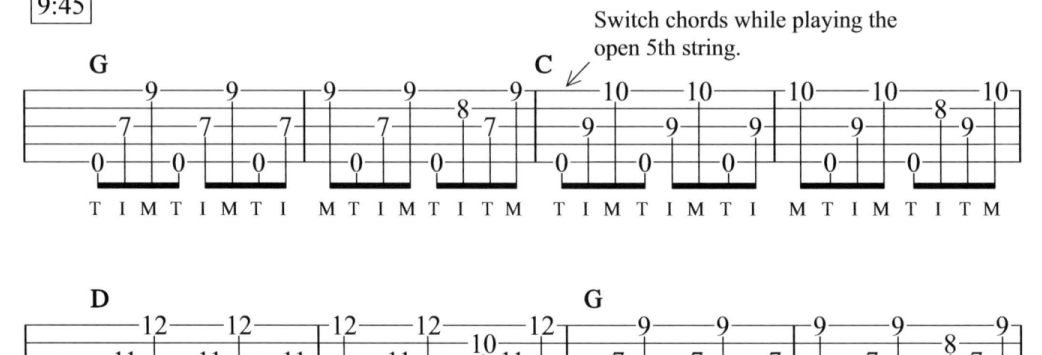

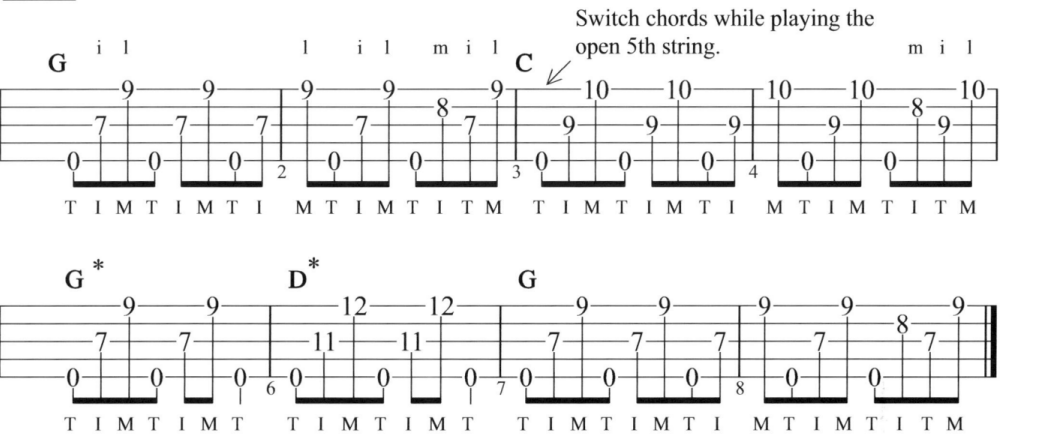

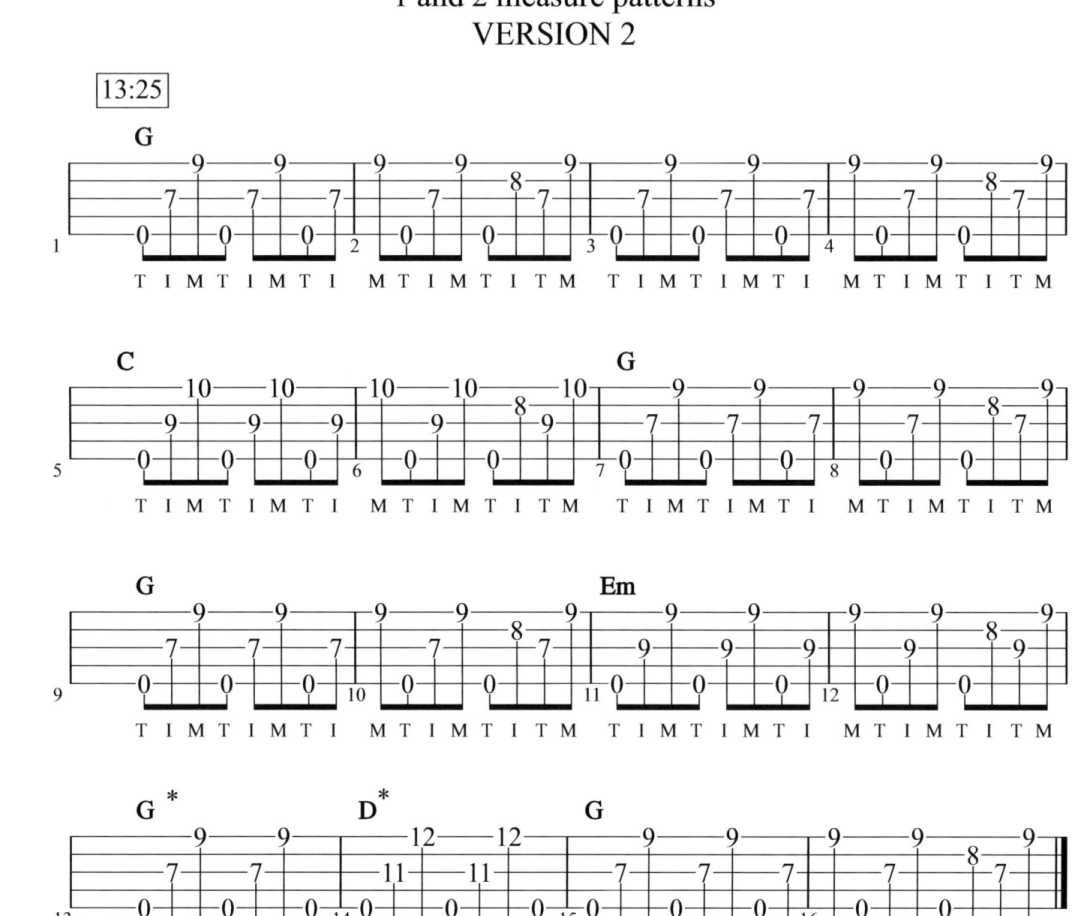

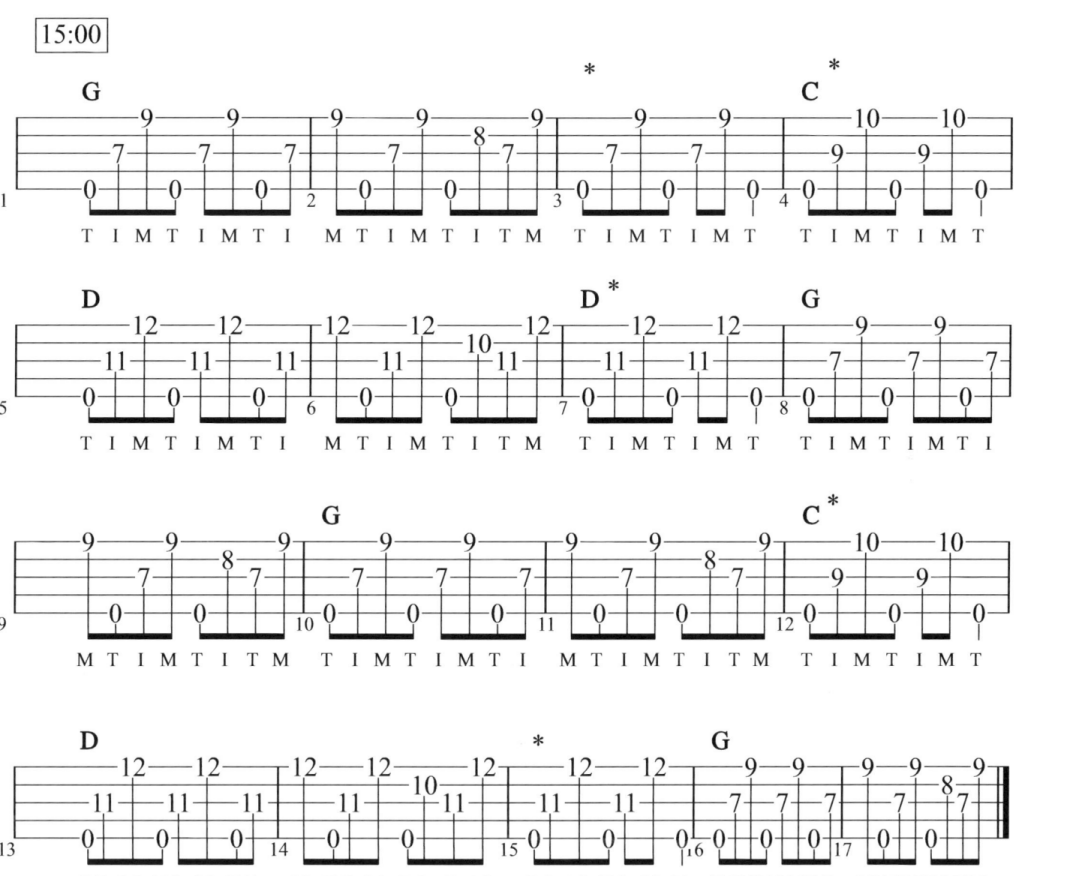

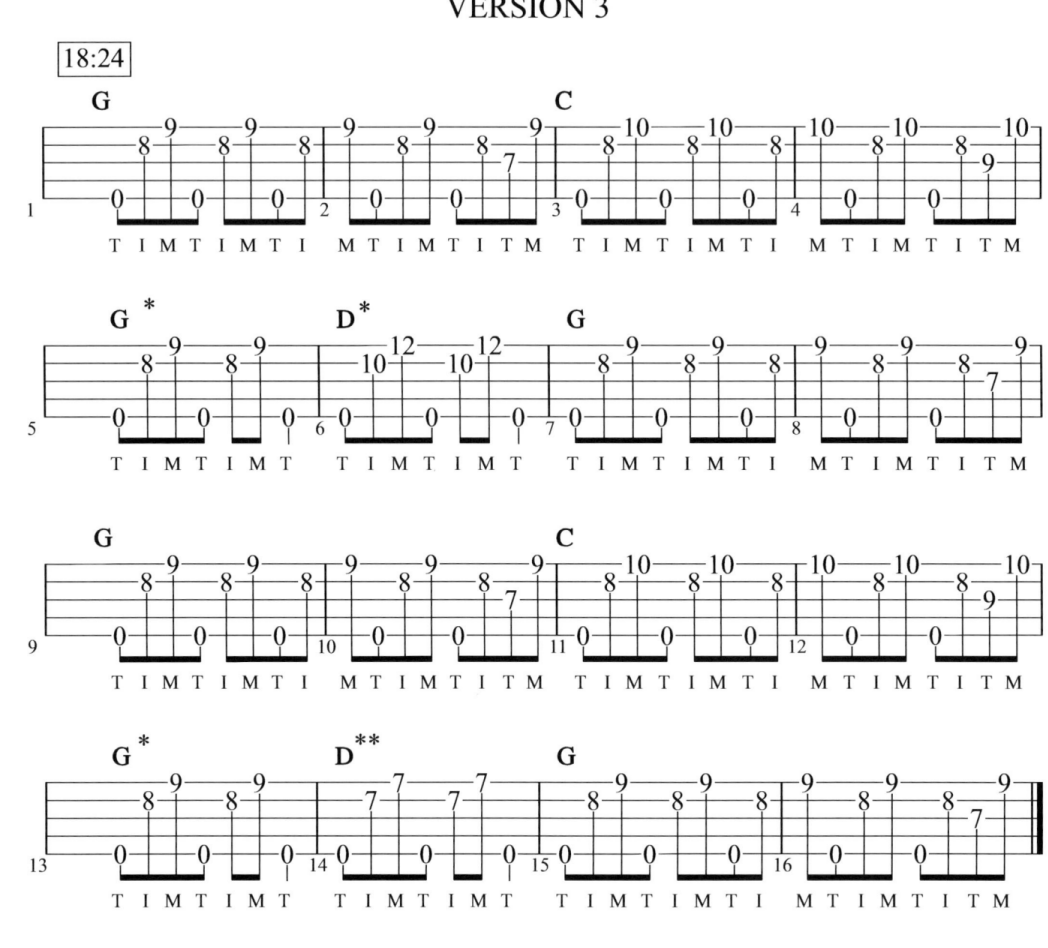

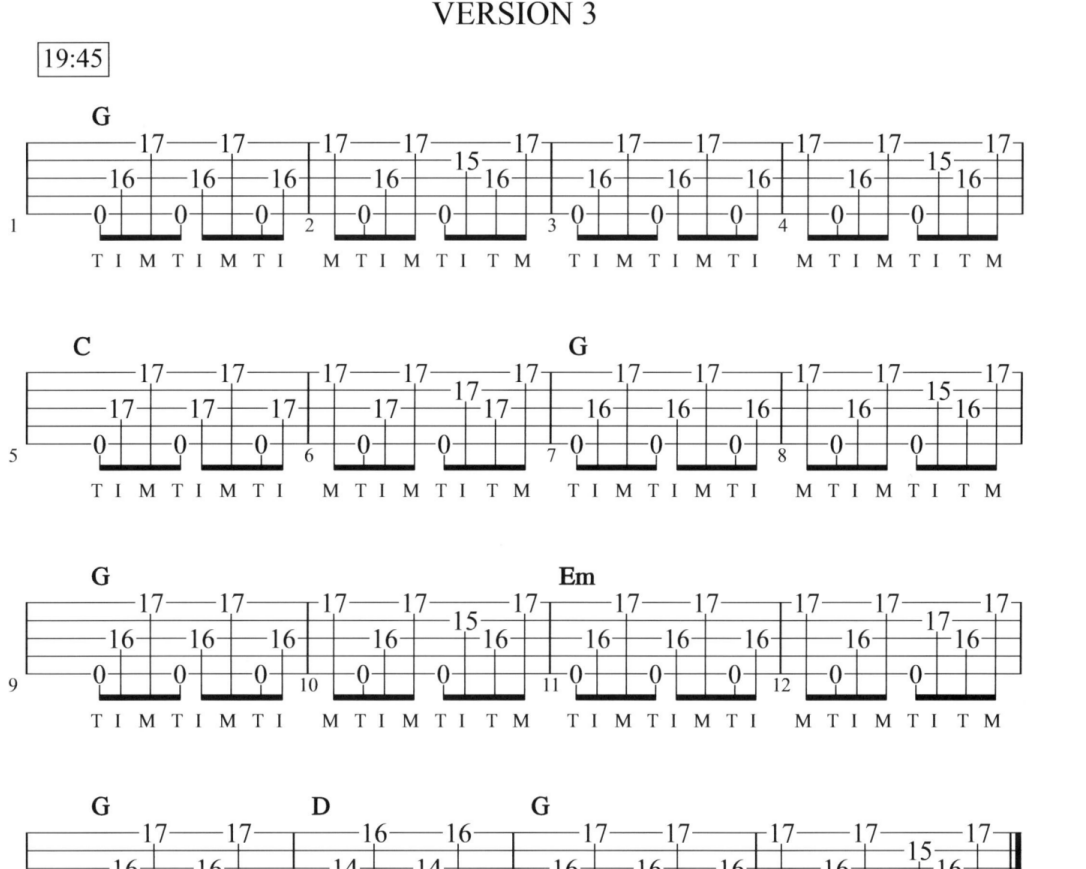

Backup Licks & Rolls Lesson 6

Section 1 - Interchangeable Backup Patterns 1-4

Pattern 1

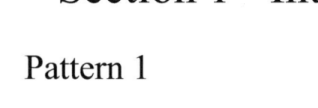

From lesson: Combining Backup Patterns

Pattern 2

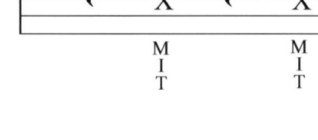

From lesson: Moveable Major Chords 3

Pattern 3

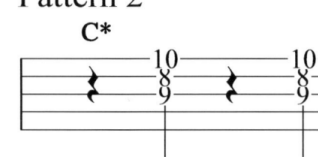

From lesson: Moveable Major Chords 3 (Same as pattern 2 with 4th string added.)

Pattern 4

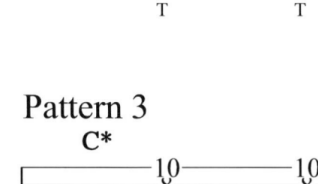

From lesson: Combining Backup Patterns

*The right hand patterns here can be used with any of the up-the-neck chords in the "Using Chord Clusters" lesson.

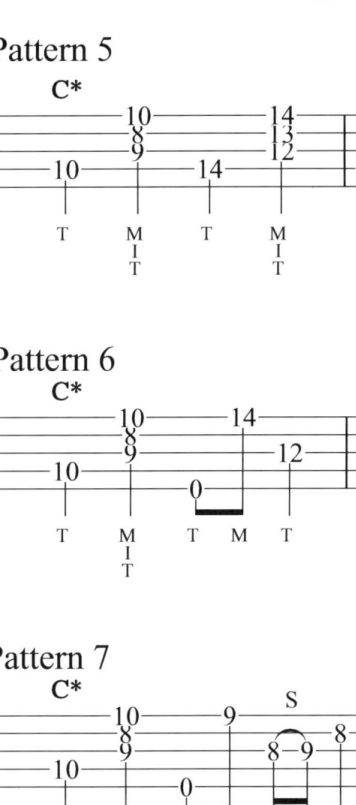

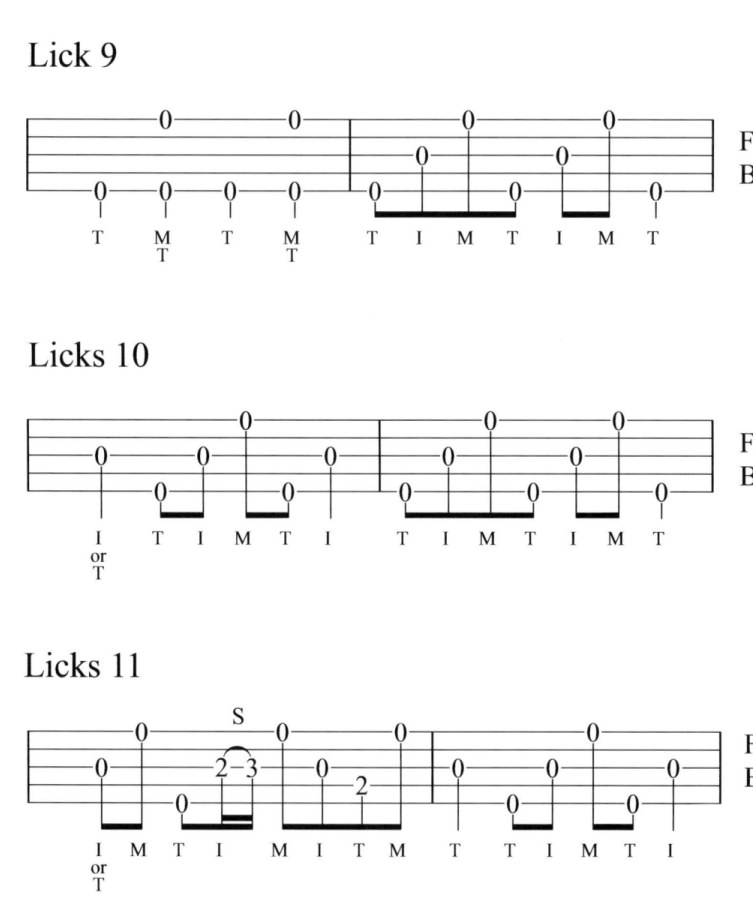

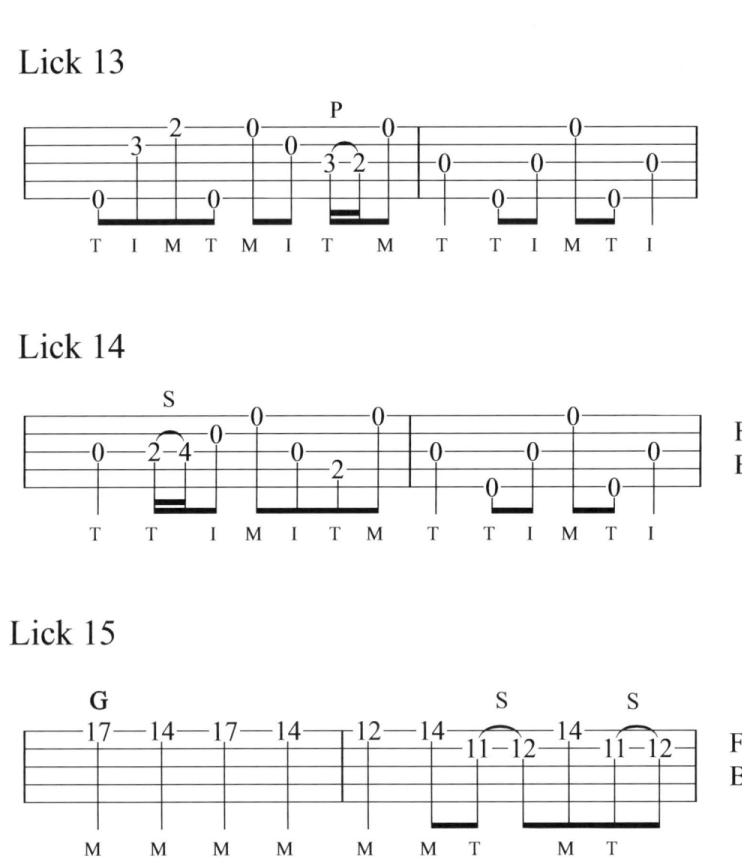

Section 2 - Mixing Backup Patterns & Licks

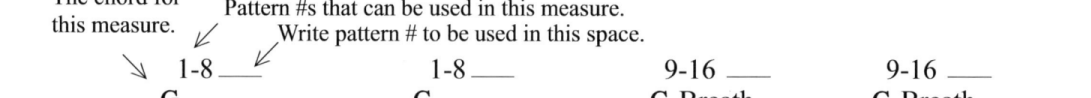

Goin' Down That Road
Examples of the First 4 Measures

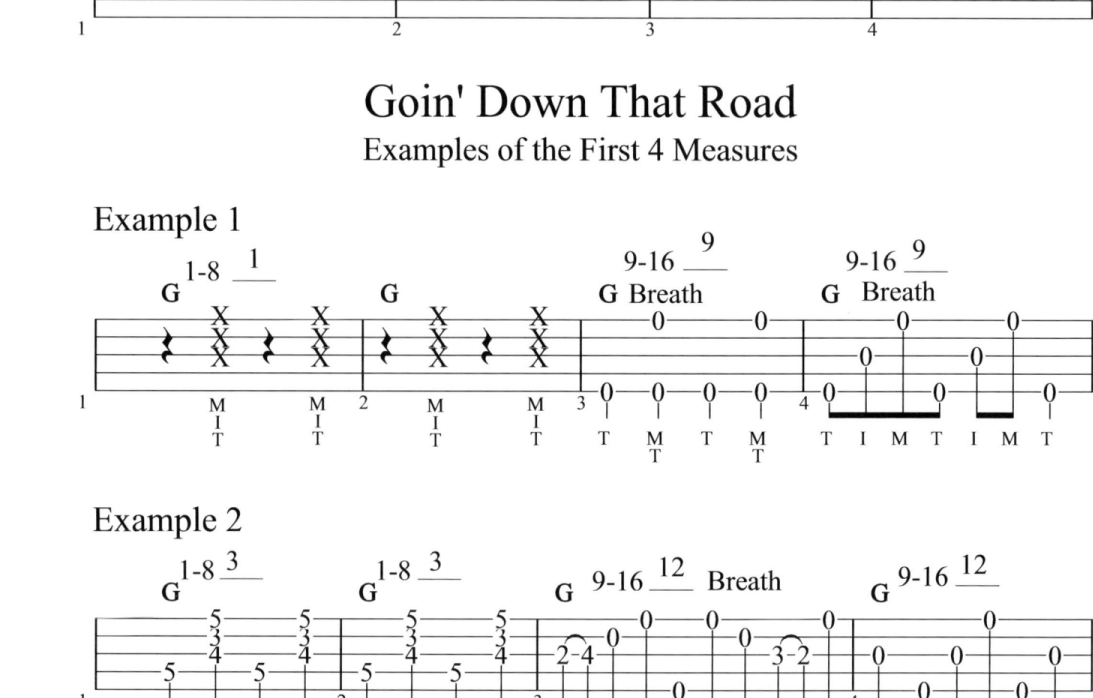

Backup Licks & Rolls 6 • Page 5

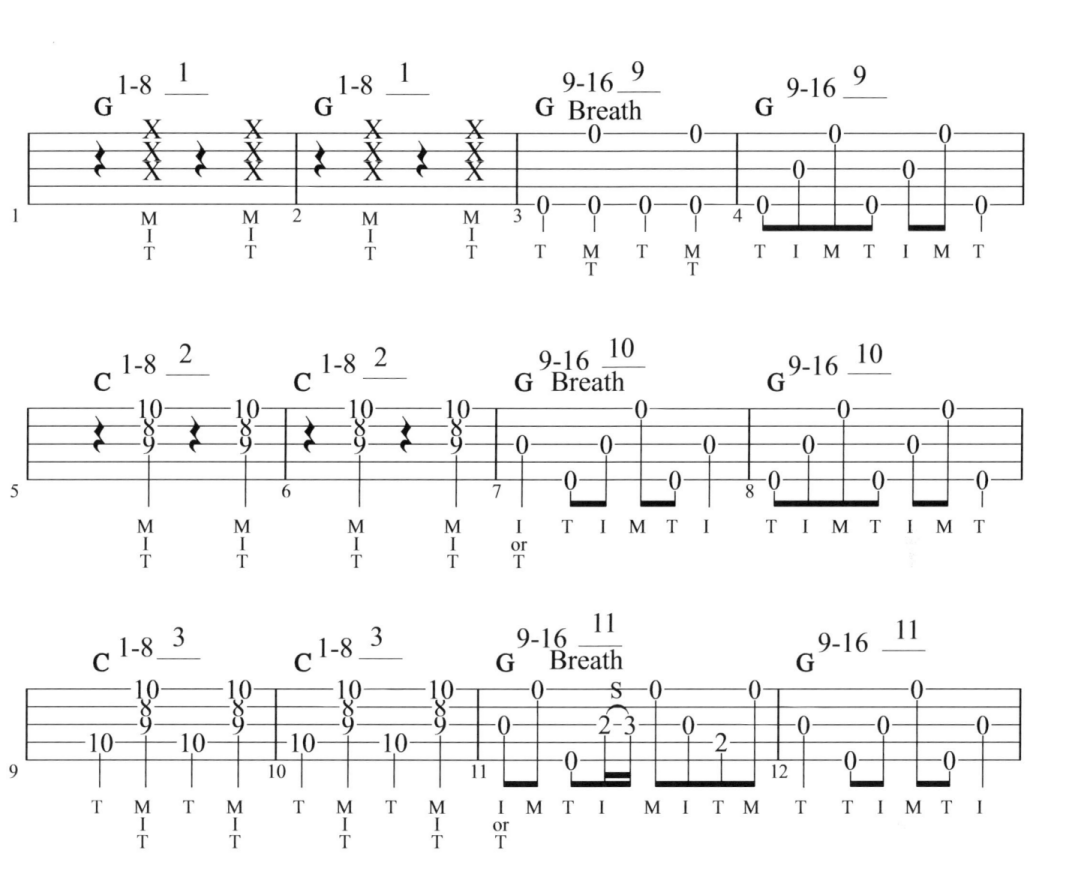

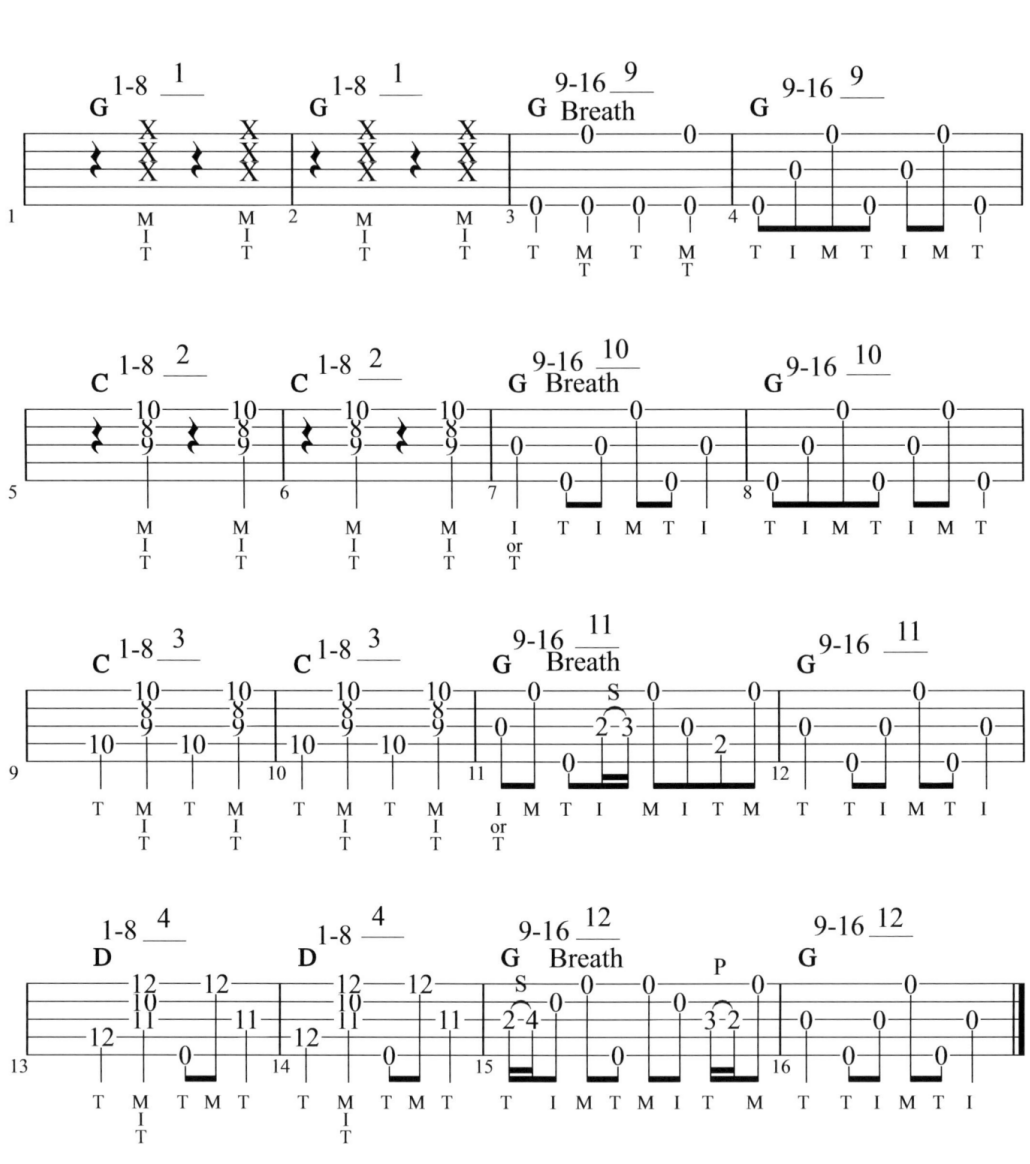

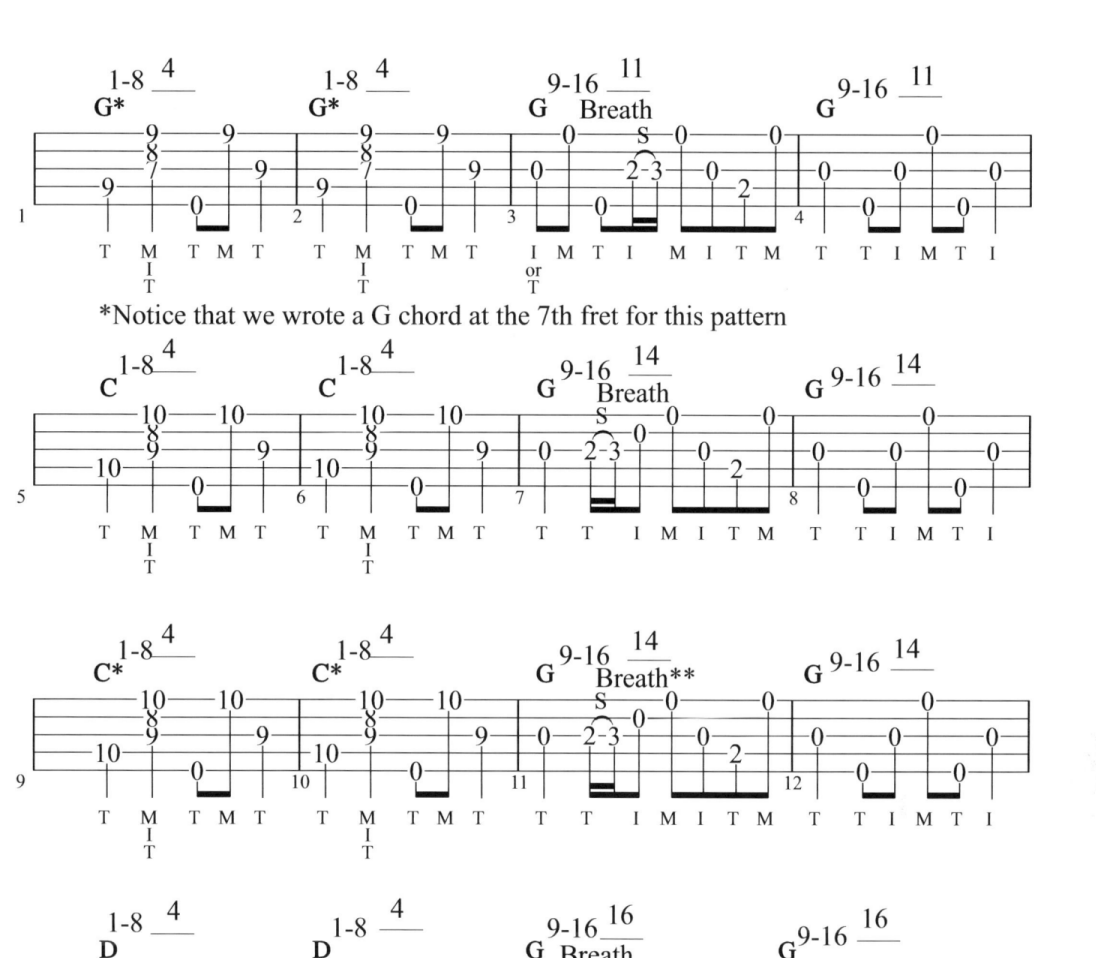

Instructions For Creating Your Own Backup

1. Go to all of the measures marked 9 through 16 in the template and write a number between 9 and 16 in the space to the right of 9 through 16. Choose any number. The numbers need to repeat for 2 measures. For example, measures 3 and 4 would have the same number, measures 7 and 8 would have the same numbers etc.

2. Go to all the spaces marked 1through 8 and write in a number 1 through 8. Once again you need to repeat the numbers for 2 measures. So, measures 1 and 2 would have the same number 5 and 6 would have the same number etc.

3. You've now chosen your patterns and licks. Using the Back Up Patterns and Licks sheets as a reference hand write in the patterns and licks you have chosen on the Goin Down That Road Template. Take your time and write clearly.

4. You now have a back up for Going Down That Road that you can play with the included MP3 tracks.

5. If the back up is too complicated or too hard, get another Back Up Template and write out another back up where the patterns and Licks repeat themselves or are easier.

6. Now practice your back up with one of the MP3 tracks.

7. As an exercise, write out a few more variations to Goin Down That Road Feeling Bad and practice them with the tracks.

Section 3 - Creating Your Own Backup
Goin' Down That Road - Template & Worksheet*

For Working Out Your Own Backup Arrangements.
Print as many copies as you need.

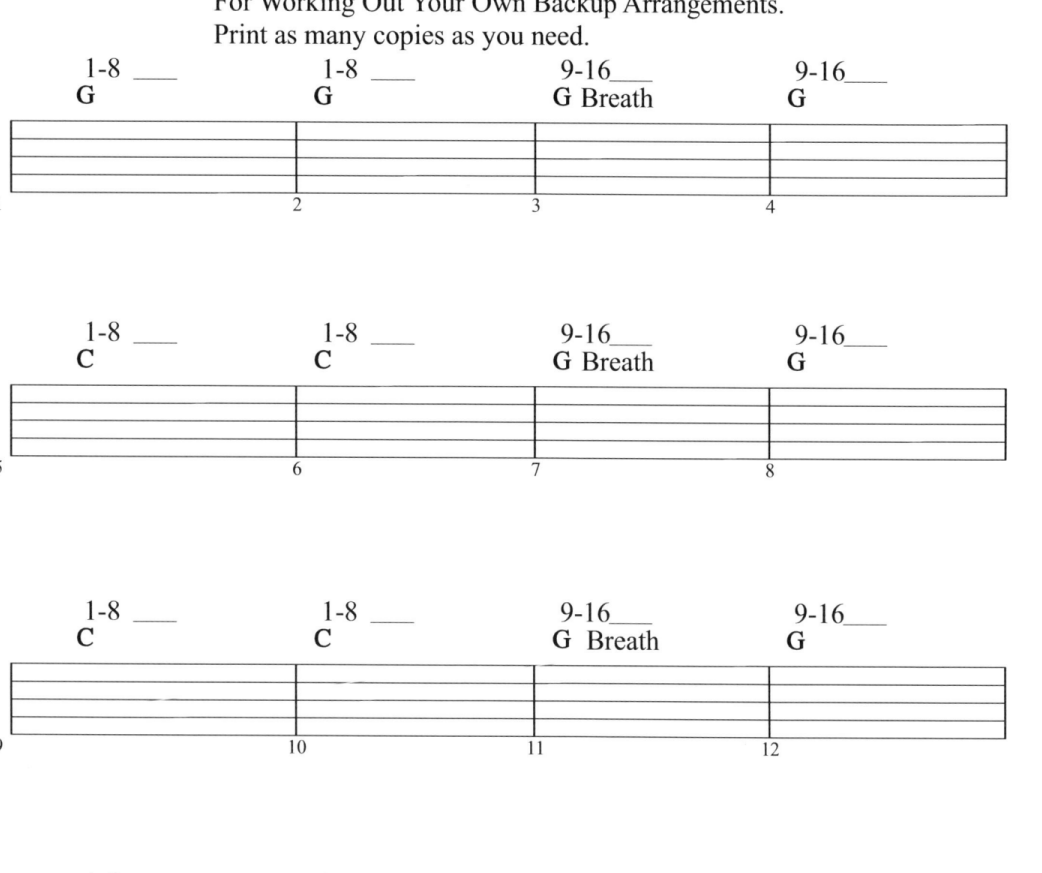

* This worksheet is completely blank.

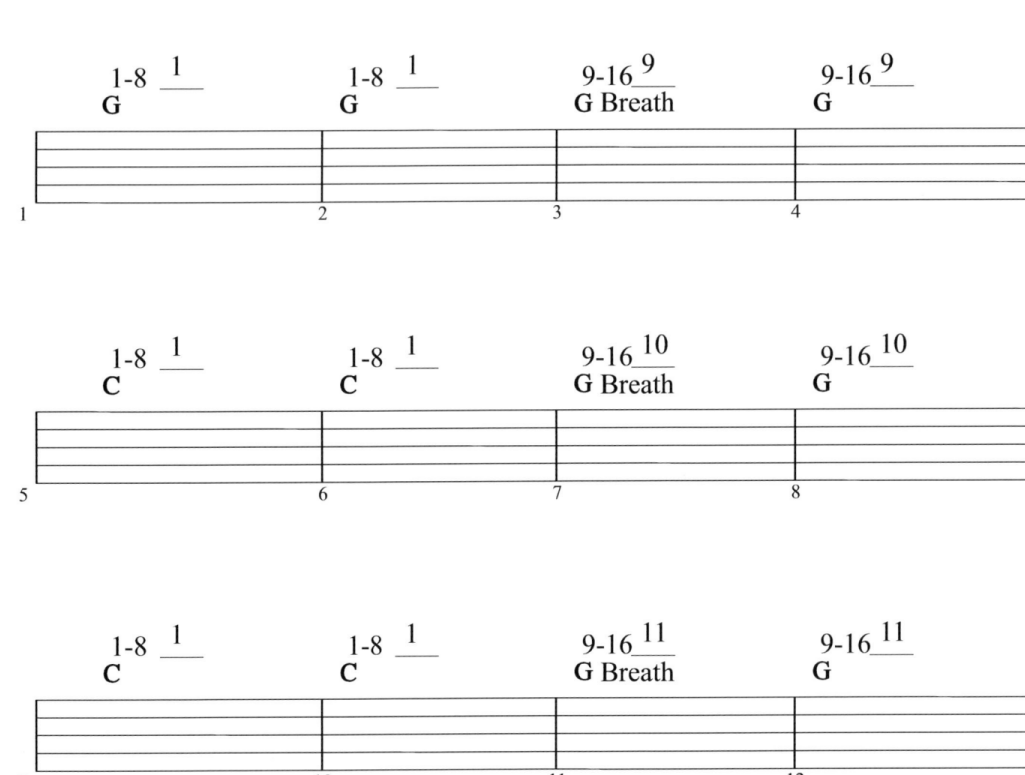

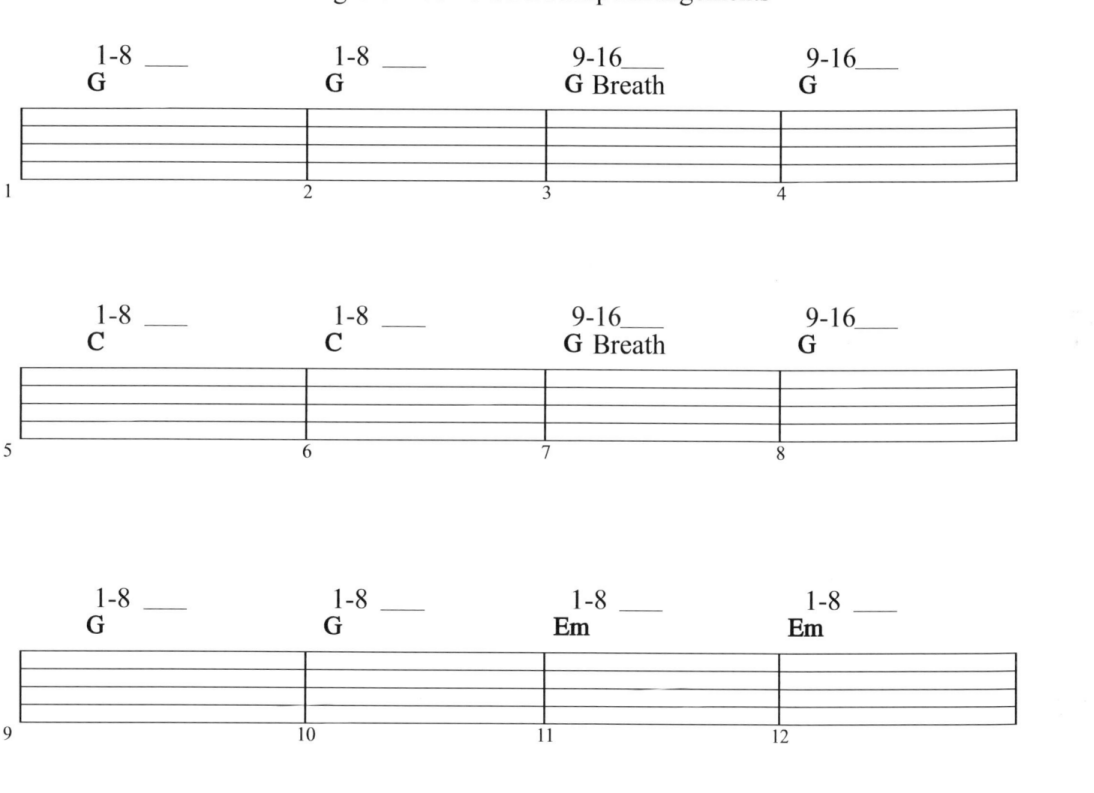

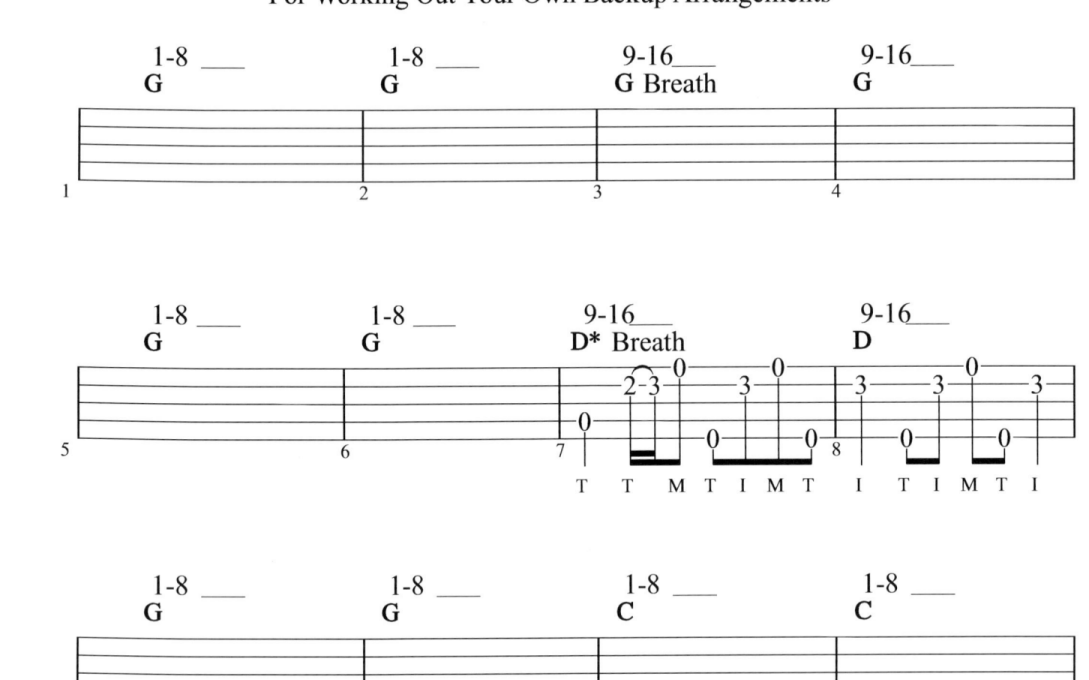

Other Banjo Products

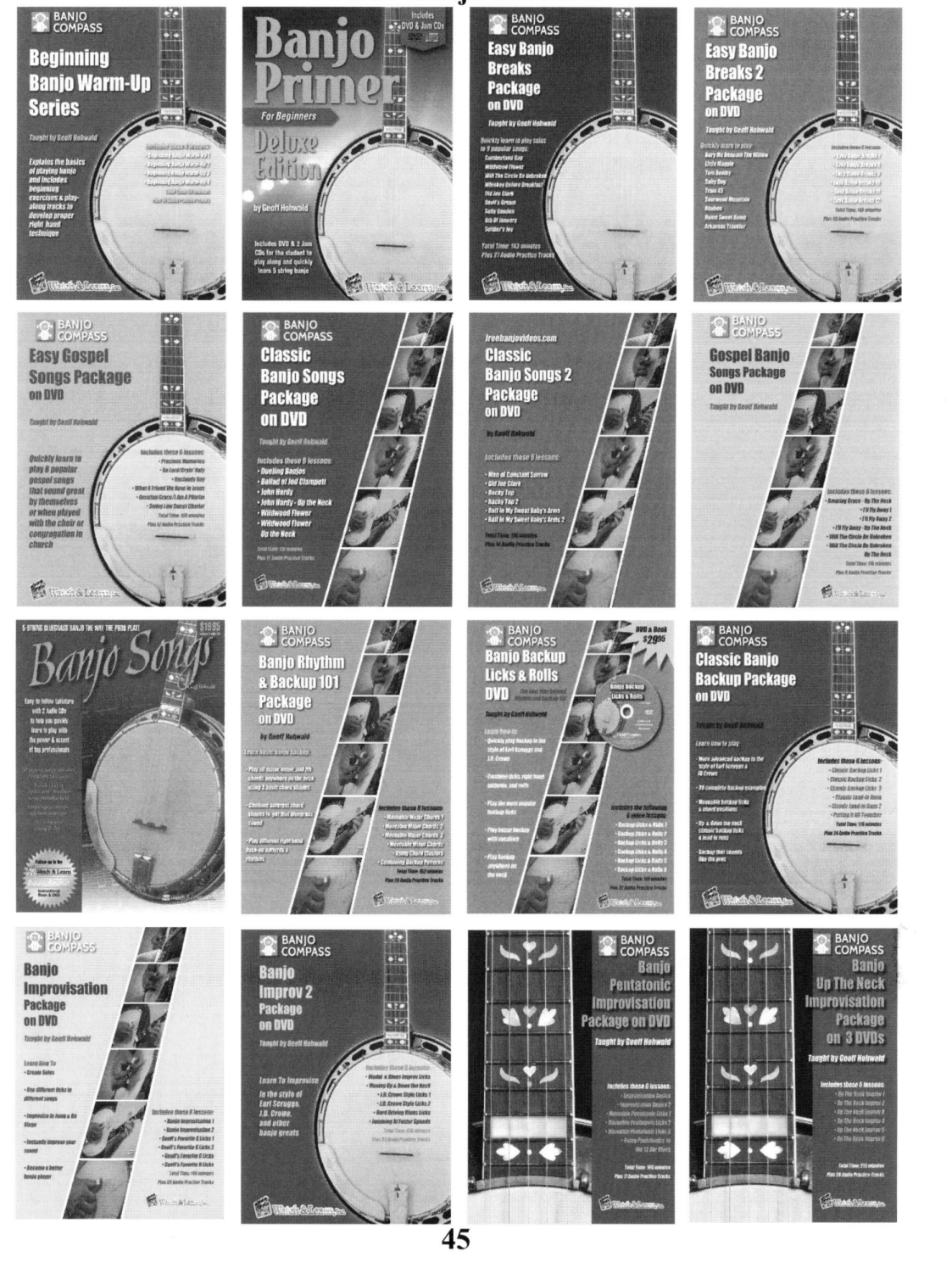

Printed in Great Britain
by Amazon